A Guide to SCOTS LAW

Richard Keith & George Clark

JOHNSTON AND BACON
LONDON AND EDINBURGH

A Johnston & Bacon book published by
Cassell Ltd.
35 Red Lion Square, London WC1R 4SG
& Tanfield House, Tanfield Lane, Edinburgh EH3 5LL
and at Sydney, Auckland, Toronto, Johannesburg,
an affiliate of Macmillan Publishing Co., Inc,
New York

First published 1978

ISBN 0 7179 4244 9

CONTENTS

INTRODUCTION

One of the ironies of democracy is that the more democratic a state becomes the more frequently laws are produced which control the lives of the individuals within that state, and the more complex these laws become. Scots law is part of Scotland's heritage and evolution, a part of which we can rightly be proud, and the Scottish legal system is held in high esteem the world over. It is not a mirror image of English law, but, as regards publications for the layman, it has tended to be ignored. Many booklets dealing with legal topics give only a passing mention to the Scottish position, and mainly concern themselves with the English approach to the law. The two systems are, however, essentially different in many respects. The primary function of this book is to provide the reader with useful information on subjects where the law is peculiar to Scotland—information which is not readily available elsewhere.

This book is not intended to be an authoritative statement of Scots law, but we hope that it will form the basis for an improved comprehension of the overall subject. We hope that the better informed reader will be more able to draw the real benefits of the legal system and of the services provided by solicitors and others. It should not be regarded as a handbook for do-it-yourself law. Law is a highly complex and technical field in which it is often extremely dangerous for unqualified persons to dabble. This does not mean that the individual should not concern himself with the law. After all, it affects virtually every step in our daily lives, but we would recommend that, if a legal problem arises, you consult a solicitor or other professional adviser at once, as he can, in most cases, more readily put things right.

The legal profession in Scotland has in recent years come under criticism for its failure to make the public fully aware of the services which a solicitor can provide. The profession is not wholly to blame for this state of affairs, as advertising by individual solicitors is prohibited, and the cost of institutional advertising is extremely high. As a result the profession has been unable to produce an image which inspires whole-hearted confidence with the public it serves. Many people feel that solicitors are too remote, and that the services they provide are bound to be prohibitively expensive. Neither of these criticisms is entirely justified, and we hope that this book will complement recent attempts to disperse the cloud of mysticism which shrouds the working of the legal profession.

Scots law is a vast subject, and it is impossible in a book of this length to cover more than a few of the areas in which the individual comes in contact with legal processes. We have, for example, covered very little of criminal law, and we do not touch at all on income tax and social security benefits which are explained in pamphlets produced by the Inland Revenue and Department of Health and Social Security.[1] We deal in turn with the family, the home and the job, and there is a section on some problems of everyday life, including consumer law and road traffic law. Some subjects undoubtedly merit greater attention than others, but we have had to balance our coverage as best we can.

Any attempt to simplify the wording of the law necessarily involves a risk that inaccuracies will result, and we cannot be held responsible to any reader who acts on the assumption that the book is a complete statement of the law. One final word of warning we would add is that the law is ever-changing, and it is always possible that the law on any topic we have covered may have altered since the time of going to print.

Throughout the book we have tried to state the law as at 31st January 1978, except where otherwise stated.

[1] You can find D.H.S.S. pamphlets at your local Post Office or Social Security Office. Inland Revenue pamphlets can be obtained from H.M. Inland Revenue, Centre I, East Kilbride, or from your local Inspector of Taxes.

HISTORY OF SCOTS LAW

There are today two major 'schools' into which the legal systems of most countries fall. The first is the Continental School which is based on the law of the Ancient Romans and its later offshoots. The legal systems of much of Western Europe, including France and Germany, and of South America, are members of this school. There are, of course, wide differences between the detail of the law in these countries, but the foundation stone is common—the methodical genius of the Roman Empire which developed a comprehensive system of law on which half the countries of the civilised world have built their domestic systems. The second school is the Common Law School which includes the systems of England, the United States, and most of the Commonwealth countries. The communist systems are sometimes said to form a third school, but are probably better regarded as a variant of the Continental system.

Scots law does not fall into either of these great schools, but stands midway between them. The fact that Scotland has an admirable system of her own devising is largely a matter of historical accident—one would have expected Scotland to develop a system very close to that south of the border. Indeed, we have borrowed much from England, but centuries of wars with the English hindered the amalgamation of the legal systems of the two countries. On the other hand, our strong contacts with Continental countries, especially France, led many of our law students to universities such as Paris, Bologna and Leiden. This and the early influence of the Canon law of the church meant that we borrowed extensively from the Roman law of the Continent. We might have continued to do so, had it not been for the work of Sir James Dalrymple, Viscount Stair (1619–95), who in 1681 published his *Institutions* which, for the first time, presented Scots law as a coherent system of principles fashioned from various sources: native custom, case law, feudal law, Roman law, Canon law, the law of nature and of the Bible. It would be difficult to overestimate the debt which Scots lawyers and the Scottish people owe to Stair. He took all these roots and moulded them into a comprehensive, rational and unique legal system, which has developed into what we now know as Scots law—a major part of our national heritage, and believed by some commentators to be an ideal model of the legal system required by modern civilised nations.

Since the time of Stair, partly as a result of the Union of the Parliaments, 1707, the influence of English law has strengthened. Improved communications and increased trading between the two countries have also contributed to this change of direction, but Scotland has preserved a system of which she is justly proud, and is today much better placed to resist any attempt at assimilation.

It is worth pausing to look briefly at the position of Scots law prior to the end of the seventeenth century. Unfortunately it is impossible to piece together with complete accuracy the history of Scots law. The Records of Scotland were twice plundered by the English, first by Edward I and then by Cromwell, and much of the historical documentation which might have given us the answers was lost forever.

Prior to 1745 there were virtually two nations in Scotland—the Lowlands on the one hand, and the Highlands and Islands on the other. By the twelfth and thirteenth centuries the Lowlands were under the influence of Anglo-Norman law. In addition they had their own customary law, and were influenced to a certain extent by Canon and Roman law. The Highlands and Islands, however, were little affected by England. There the influence of Celtic law was still very strong, and traces of Celtic law persisted for long north of the Forth and Clyde, largely due to the clan structure of society.

We are unable to assess accurately the historical importance of Celtic law in Scotland, but it is clear that it has had very little influence on modern Scots law. Much better authenticated is the influence of Anglo-Norman law and the feudal system which seems to have reached us from England. Feudalism in Scotland was developing in the early twelfth century. It formed a means whereby the king could extend his power in a country where he had not yet succeeded in establishing effective government.

By the reign of David I (1124–53) a Sheriff represented the king at strategic centres. The Sheriff administered justice in the king's name—the beginning of the modern Sheriff Court. Only when the king effectively controlled and governed most of the country could a centralised court be effective, and in the thirteenth century Scotland lagged far behind England in this process. A certain amount of customary law was growing up by this time and efforts to increase the prominence of statute law were being made. The Wars of Independence interrupted this development, and with the loss of the Records of Scotland it is impossible to tell what the position was by the early fourteenth century. One document which has survived is an early compilation of laws called the *Regiam Majestatem*. This is obviously based on an English tract, and the compiler may simply have edited it to take account of the difference at that time between the laws of Lowland Scotland and England. This suggests that the two systems were very similar when the *Regiam Majestatem* was compiled, but historians have been unable to date the work with certainty. The current view is that it may have been an attempt to rebuild the system after the Wars of Independence. If so, it indicates that even in the fourteenth century the two systems coincided on many important points.

The *Regiam Majestatem* had an enormous influence on Scots law. By 1425 it was clearly in need of revision, for there is an Act of Parliament of James I setting up a Commission to examine and amend it as required. In this later mediaeval period much important legislation was passed, including, in 1424, the beginning of a legal assistance scheme for persons unable to pay legal fees.

There followed an era of increasing Roman influence, partly through Canon law and then through the fifteenth-century revival of interest in Roman law which led many Scots students to study law on the Continent. The foundation in 1532 of the centralised Court of Session, with its permanent judiciary, accelerated this process, as in the reported cases the judges referred to Roman law to support many of their judgments. Then in 1681 the publication of Stair's work halted the reception of Roman law into Scotland. The Union with England resulted in civil appeals going beyond the Court of Session to the House of Lords, and in legislation being passed for both countries, and the English influence was increased. The numbers of Scottish students abroad declined and was finally abruptly halted by the Napoleonic Wars (1793–1815). It is true to say, however, that complete areas of modern Scots law owe a large debt to Roman law, and many Latin words and phrases are still used in our legal textbooks and in the courts.

In the last 150 years or so the national law of Scotland has developed by its own vitality. Much improved systems of reporting cases, which can be used as precedents in future litigation, have played a large part in this development. The main external influence is now English law which infiltrates by means of Acts of Parliament, which, while in accord with English legal principles, are sometimes at variance with those of Scotland. Scots law is also shaped by decisions of the House of Lords in Scottish appeals, where only a minority of the Lords who hear appeals are trained in Scots law.

Modern Sources of Scots Law

Case Law

The layman could be forgiven for thinking of 'law' in terms of celebrated murder trials when the criminal is brought to justice, after which the rest of the community can breathe more easily. Equally, he could be excused if he asserted that all law was contained in Acts of Parliament. He gains this impression through the media. The popular press reports widely trials which it considers to be of public interest and the parliamentary debates over government legislation. In fact, the bulk of Scots law is neither legislation nor criminal law, but what is called case law. Whenever a judge or Sheriff pronounces his findings, he is influencing the development of the law on the point at issue. His decision has to be followed by all lower courts if the same point is disputed at a future date. It is common for a litigant to argue that a previous decision which does not favour his case should not be followed, as the facts of the present case are materially different. The judge or Sheriff may or may not agree, but his judgment will concern the application of the law to this new set of facts, and so the law is further developed.

Legislation

The second main source of Scots law is legislation. Prior to the Union of the Parliaments Scotland had her own legislature. Since 1707 many of the Acts of the old Scots parliament have been repealed, although some still survive. Added to these is the enormous mass of legislation of the United Kingdom parliament, in so far as that legislation refers to Scotland. Legislation is ever-changing to take account of alterations in approach by successive governments and shifting social attitudes. It is concerned with the detailed legal regulation of our lives, and it is an important source of law, even although large areas of law are not regulated to any great extent by statute.

When we talk of the 'common law', we are referring mainly to law which is not the product of an Act of Parliament.

Due to the difference between the legal systems of Scotland and England, many Acts of the United Kingdom parliament apply to Scotland alone. Scotland, however, has only seventy-one Members of Parliament, and only one-tenth of the population of England and Wales. It is inevitable, though regrettable, that only a fraction of parliamentary time can be devoted to purely Scottish affairs. The consequences of this for Scots law are only too clear. Principles of English law, entirely alien to our system, may be introduced into Scotland simply by the extension to Scotland of Acts of Parliament prepared in London by parliamentary draftsmen experienced primarily in English law. This creates serious problems of interpretation for the courts in Scotland when questions arise as to the precise meaning of such Acts. The other consequence for Scotland is that much-needed legal reform on purely Scottish matters may take many years due to the pressure on the government's legislative programme. Divorce law reform is the most obvious recent example. The government could not find time to include it in their legislative schedule, and it took several unsuccessful attempts before a Bill to reform Scottish divorce law came high on the ballot for Private Members' Bills, and eventually became the Divorce (Scotland) Act 1976. A Scottish Assembly may help to improve this unfortunate state of affairs.

Legislation, as a source of law, may take the form either of

Acts of Parliament, or of what is called 'subordinate legislation'. The latter comprises mainly statutory instruments, which are regulations made by a government minister, and bye-laws, which are made by local authorities or public authorities and are of local effect. There is an enormous mass of subordinate legislation, which must be made under powers conferred on local or public authorities, or on a certain government minister, by an Act of Parliament. For example, the Local Government (Scotland) Act 1973 could not possibly have contained all the detailed regulations relating to the workings of local authorities and their departments. The Act therefore contained clauses empowering individual local authorities to make their own regulations under the Act. In our section on hire purchase we will see that there are now minimum deposits and maximum repayment periods. These are not mentioned in the Hire Purchase (Scotland) Act 1965, but are part of The Hire-Purchase And Credit Sale Agreements (Control) Order 1976[1] which is a statutory instrument made by the Secretary of State for Prices and Consumer Protection. This power was conferred on the Secretary by the Emergency Laws (Re-Enactments and Repeals) Act 1964.

Institutional Writers

The third major source of Scots law is found in the works of the 'Institutional Writers'. Writers of legal textbooks may attain a reputation so high that their works acquire authority, and if there is no case law or statute relating to a particular issue, the courts will turn to the views of these writers. We have already mentioned Lord Stair's contribution to Scots law, but he is not the only writer whose views are still looked to in the twentieth century. Others of importance are Baron Hume (1756–1838), the first to systematise Scottish criminal law, and Erskine (1695–1768) and Bell (1770–1843). It is surprising how often Institutional Writers are still referred to in court, even though it is in some cases nearly three hundred years since their works were first published. Social and economic conditions change with time but basic legal principles alter little over the years, so the authoritative value of writers such as Stair continues.

[1] 1976 S.I. 1135

Canon Law

The Christian church in Western Europe, particularly the Roman Church, developed an extensive system called the Canon law. This had a wide influence, especially on the law relating to the family, but after the Reformation of 1560 the church courts of the Middle Ages disappeared and their powers on matters of marriage, legitimacy and succession were taken over by the Scottish secular courts. The importance of Canon law has largely been overshadowed by other modern sources of law, but, until 31st December 1977, Scots lawyers still had to look to the Book of Leviticus, chapter 18, for prohibited degrees of relationship as a bar to marriage. Canon law was largely based on Roman law, and church courts were, until the twelfth and thirteenth centuries, far more important than lay courts.

Custom

Custom plays only a very small part as a separate source of law. Many of the older customs have been embodied in Acts of Parliament and judicial decisions in court cases, and have become part of the general common law of Scotland. There is now no separate body of 'customary law' as such. A particular custom derived its authority as law from its continued use and recognition by the community.

These then are the main sources of modern Scots law. It will be clear that the law is not static, but is ever-changing to take account of altering social attitudes and government policies, and that the various sources are constantly interacting.

THE STRUCTURE OF THE SYSTEM

Scots law divides basically into two major divisions – civil law and criminal law.

Civil law, which we will deal with later, is concerned with the enforcement of private rights and obligations between individuals. Criminal law covers all acts and omissions which may be the subject of prosecution in the criminal courts, and which may lead to punishments such as fines or imprisonment for those found guilty. Prosecutions in criminal law are normally brought by the state, in the interests of the community as a whole.

Criminal law developed from the need for maintenance of peace, security and stability in society as a whole. When a system of government has been established to represent and implement these collective aims, criminal law fixes the limits of state interest in the doings of individuals, and provides the machinery for dealing with those who transgress these limits.

Criminal Law

The system of criminal prosecution has at its head the Lord Advocate, who is appointed by the Prime Minister. He is the legal representative of the Crown in Scotland, and an experienced advocate, usually a Member of Parliament (assuming there is an advocate in the government party). He is responsible to parliament for his decision whether or not to prosecute any particular case. The Lord Advocate, in turn, appoints the Solicitor-General, the second law officer of the Crown, and several Advocates-Depute, who conduct the High Court trials throughout Scotland. The necessary administrative machinery is provided by the Crown Office in Edinburgh which is staffed by civil servants.

At local level, public prosecution in the Sheriff Court and District Court is conducted by Procurators Fiscal. They are full-time civil servants who have been experienced advocates or, more usually, solicitors. They receive police reports of crimes in their Sheriffdoms, and decide whether or not to prosecute. They have to report more serious crimes to the Crown Office, to whose control they are subject. If the matter is serious enough for a High Court trial, the Fiscal will assist at, but not conduct, the trial. The Procurator Fiscal also undertakes in Scotland the functions performed by the Coroner in England; he investigates the causes of any sudden or suspicious deaths in his Sheriffdom, and initiates, where necessary, enquiries into fatal accidents.

The system of prosecution is basically public. Private prosecutions are extremely rare, and all recent attempts by individuals to raise private prosecutions have failed. The Lord Advocate must consent to a private prosecution. If he refuses to consent, a petition called a Bill for Criminal Letters can be presented to the High Court. The last case in which such a petition succeeded was in 1909, so for all practical purposes it can be assumed that if the Lord Advocate declines to prosecute in any case, that is the end of the matter.

The Criminal Courts

The High Court of Justiciary

This is the highest criminal court in Scotland where trials for the most serious crimes are heard. The High Court does not sit only in Edinburgh, but goes on circuit to Aberdeen, Ayr, Dumfries, Dundee, Glasgow, Inverness, Jedburgh, Oban, Perth and Stirling. It has the exclusive right to hear certain cases: in particular, murder, treason, rape and incest. Most trials in the High Court are heard by one judge with a jury of fifteen persons. This is called 'solemn procedure'. The charge is contained in a document called an Indictment. Solemn procedure is contrasted with 'summary procedure' when the judge sits alone without a jury. In solemn procedure the judge decides questions of law and directs the jury accordingly. The jury have the task of deciding questions of fact on hearing the evidence. A simple majority of eight to seven is sufficient for a verdict of guilty. In summary procedure, the judge or Sheriff decides both questions of law and fact, unaided by a jury.

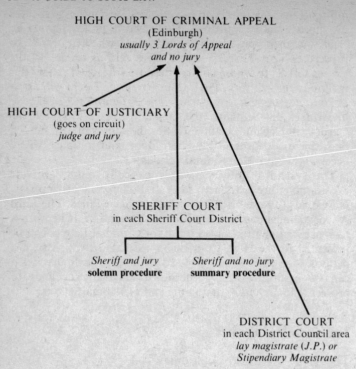

HIGH COURT OF CRIMINAL APPEAL
(Edinburgh)
*usually 3 Lords of Appeal
and no jury*

HIGH COURT OF JUSTICIARY
(goes on circuit)
judge and jury

SHERIFF COURT
in each Sheriff Court District

Sheriff and jury
solemn procedure

Sheriff and no jury
summary procedure

DISTRICT COURT
in each District Council area
*lay magistrate (J.P.) or
Stipendiary Magistrate*

*Diagram showing the structure of the criminal courts in Scotland
Arrows indicate the lines of appeal*

The High Court has unlimited powers of sentence. Although murder is no longer punishable by death, the High Court can still impose the death penalty on persons found guilty of treason. The sentence for murder is now compulsorily fixed at life imprisonment, and it is quite common for Acts of Parliament to set out maximum sentences for various offences; but, with these exceptions, the High Court is free to punish by admonition (i.e. warning), fine, probation or imprisonment.

The High Court also sits as a court of appeal when there are usually three judges and no jury. Appeals may come from the High, Sheriff or District Court. In such cases it sits as the High Court of Criminal Appeal.

The Sheriff Court

Scotland is divided into six Sheriffdoms, which, in turn, sub-divide into fifty districts, each of which has its own Sheriff Court. The Sheriffdoms correspond to groupings of the local authority regions with the exception of Strathclyde Region, which, because of its size, is divided between three Sheriffdoms. From north to south the Sheriffdoms are:

1 Grampian, Highland and Islands.
2 Tayside, Central and Fife.
3 Lothian and Borders.
4 North Strathclyde.
5 Glasgow and Strathkelvin.
6 South Strathclyde, Dumfries and Galloway.

Glasgow has by far the busiest Sheriff Court in Scotland, and the largest volume of criminal and civil cases. The bulk of the Sheriff Court's criminal business takes the form of summary trials, but it also has solemn jurisdiction, which means that the Sheriff tries cases with a jury. The Sheriff does not hear criminal appeals from lower courts. These go directly to the High Court of Justiciary.

The sentencing powers of the Sheriff are limited to two years' imprisonment, if procedure is by indictment (jury trial), and three months' in a summary case. For a small group of offences involving dishonesty or personal violence, if the accused has a previous conviction for a similar offence, the Sheriff's sentencing power in a summary trial is up to three months in prison. There is no limit to the Sheriff's power to impose fines in cases under solemn procedure, but in summary cases the usual limit is £1000. The Sheriff has the power to send a case to the High Court for sentence if it merits a penalty more severe than he can impose. An appeal from the Sheriff Court goes to the High Court.

The District Court

As a result of local government reorganisation in 1975, regions were subdivided into districts and certain Islands authorities were also created. These geographical and administrative divisions form the basis of the District Courts which take the place of the old Burgh Courts and Justice of the

Peace Courts. The District Courts deal with minor criminal offences such as breach of the peace. They do not hear any civil cases. The procedure is always summary, and generally the maximum sentencing powers are sixty days' imprisonment and fines not exceeding £200. There is no appeal from the District Court to the Sheriff Court—any appeal is direct to the High Court of Justiciary.

Civil Law

Civil law divides into public law and private law. Public law regulates the functions of the state and the organisation of our political and social system. Private law, with which we are concerned, regulates the rights and obligations between individuals, and provides the citizen with a means of redress, in particular, the right to compensation, for wrongs done to him. Private law subdivides informally into several major areas:

(a) Family law, including marriage, divorce, custody and guardianship of children, and adoption.
(b) Law of contract, including sale of goods, hire purchase, employment, partnerships.
(c) Law of property, including disputes as to ownership or rights of possession.
(d) Law of delict (often called reparation), including actions for personal injury or damage to property caused by another's negligence, and actions of defamation where an award of damages is sought.

In later chapters we shall discuss several of these topics.

The Civil Courts

The Court of Session

The supreme civil court in Scotland is the Court of Session, founded in 1532. It sits solely in Edinburgh, in Parliament House behind St Giles' Cathedral. Cases are heard by a judge sitting alone in what is called the Outer House. Any appeal goes to one of the two Divisions of the Inner House of eight senior judges. Very occasionally, the judge sits with a jury of

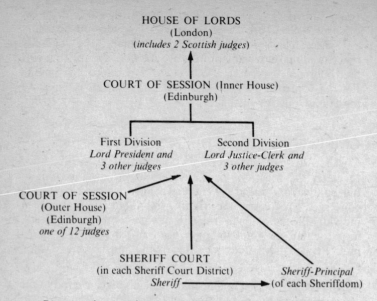

Diagram showing the structure of the civil courts in Scotland
Arrows indicate the lines of appeal

twelve. The largest volume of work handled by the Outer House judges is the disposal of the eight thousand or more divorce cases per year, as divorce cases can only be heard in the Court of Session. The court also has the exclusive right in various other types of action. Cases of damages for personal injury are second most common. The Court of Session has no jurisdiction over actions for recovery of debts not exceeding £50—the Sheriff Court has the exclusive right to hear such cases.

The court has an important right, called the *nobile officium*, to provide a remedy where the existing law does not provide one, or where injustice would result from the strict application of the existing law. Today this power would only be used in very exceptional circumstances.

The Inner House hears appeals from the Sheriff Court or from the Outer House. Appeals against decisions of the Inner House can only be heard by the House of Lords in London. Such appeals are few, due to the astronomical costs involved.

Procedure

The parties to a civil action are called the pursuer (the person who raises the action) and the defender (*not* defendant). The action begins when the pursuer, usually through his solicitor, sends by recorded delivery a copy of a summons to the defender. This sets out his claim, outlines the facts on which it is based, and states the remedies which he seeks. It also warns the defender that if he does not intimate to the court, within a certain time limit, his intention to defend the action, the court will grant decree to the pursuer, that is, decide in his favour. The defender is held by his absence to have admitted the claim. The defender, through his solicitor, can lodge defences to the claim. The parties then adjust these written pleadings in the light of what the other has said, in order that the court's time need not be wasted hearing evidence on matters on which the parties are agreed. The system of written pleading highlights the real points at issue between the parties, and gives the defender full notice of the case he is required to answer. At the proof, or hearing, the parties cannot introduce evidence on matters which are not covered by their written pleadings.

When the process of adjustment is completed, a date is fixed for the proof. The parties and any other witnesses must attend the proof. Only advocates can prepare summonses, defences and adjustments in Court of Session actions (see p. 23). They, and not solicitors, appear in court on your behalf at the proof, or on any occasion prior to the proof. Such earlier appearance might occur in a divorce action, if the pursuer is trying to obtain from her husband interim aliment (financial support pending the outcome of the action), interim interdict (to keep her husband away from her) or interim custody of the children. Applications such as these come before the court as 'Motions'. The advocate and instructing solicitor appear on behalf of the parties, who need not be present, as generally no evidence is led.

The Sheriff Court

At local level this court handles the large majority of civil cases in Scotland. It can hear all cases except those exclusively reserved to the Court of Session, such as actions affecting personal status and actions of divorce. The Sheriff Court alone can hear cases where the sum sued for is below £50. A large part of the civil work of the Sheriff Court is the disposal of cases called 'Summary Causes', which are mainly actions of damages or for payment of money of a value up to £500, where the procedure is simpler than in other actions.

Procedure

Civil procedure in the Sheriff Court is broadly similar to that in the Court of Session. The document which begins the action is called an Initial Writ instead of a summons. The main difference is that in the Court of Session when the *induciae* (the period of time within which the defender must intimate to the court his intention to defend the action) has expired, it is up to the pursuer, through his solicitor, to take the next step, or nothing further happens. In an ordinary action in the Sheriff Court when the *induciae* expires, the case automatically appears on the Court Roll on a particular day. If on that day the pursuer is not represented, the action is dismissed; if the defender is not represented, decree is awarded against him in his absence. If he has intimated his intention to defend, the court will continue the action until a specified date, and order the defender to lodge written defences by a certain day. The defender should be present or represented to know whether such an order has been made and what the important dates are. If he does not lodge defences within the time limit, decree in his absence will again be awarded against him. In other words, time limits control the length of time which will elapse before a case reaches the stage of a proof. In the Court of Session, however, nothing happens unless one or other of the parties makes a move.

Procedure in Summary Causes in the Sheriff Court is different from that in ordinary actions. Summary Cause procedure is designed to provide a quick and easy way to settle disputes which it has not been possible to settle out of court. The Summons is a printed form, on which the pursuer fills in the blanks. It contains two other portions, one of which the defender must complete and return to the court by a specified date if he intends to defend the action, and the other of which he must complete and return if he admits the claim, but wishes to pay the sum sued for, plus expenses, by instalments. See also p. 142.

Further Reading

The Legal System of Scotland—H.M.S.O. (Second edition 1977)
£1.00

The Scottish Legal Tradition—Saltire Society (Fourth edition
1977) 50p

PERSONNEL OF THE LAW

The Judiciary

The High Court of Justiciary

The judges in the High Court and the Court of Session are the same people, but with different titles depending on whether they are hearing a criminal or a civil case. The High Court has at its head the Lord Justice-General, and next in importance is the Lord Justice-Clerk. The other judges are known as Lords Commissioners of Justiciary. Usually only one judge hears criminal cases, but if a trial raises difficult questions of law there may be more than one judge. It is rare for more than seven judges to hear any one case, but there have been instances where all of the judges have crammed into the High Court.

The total number of judges used to be fifteen, but it has gradually increased to twenty-one. One judge acts as Chairman of the Scottish Law Commission, a body which reviews Scots law and makes recommendations for reform to the government. There are also two Scottish judges in the Judicial Committee of the House of Lords, appointed on the recommendation of the Prime Minister. They hear appeals from Scotland on civil matters. In the High Court of Criminal Appeal a minimum of three judges hear each appeal from the High, Sheriff or District Courts. In criminal cases, there is no further appeal to the House of Lords.

Judges are usually appointed from the senior members of the Bar. The only exceptions occur when the Prime Minister or Secretary of State recommends to the Sovereign that either the Lord Advocate or the Solicitor-General be elevated to the Bench. The Prime Minister makes recommendations for the appointment of the Lord Justice-General or Lord Justice-Clerk; other judges are appointed on the recommendation of the Secretary of State for Scotland. In practice, the Lord Advocate is always consulted before a recommendation is made to the Sovereign. There is no training as such for judges, although some have been Sheriffs Principal. All will have a wide experience from appearing before the court as advocates.

Judges hold office for life unless they do something to justify their removal from the Bench, but they now retire at seventy-five. While on the Bench they must not hold political appointments or involve themselves in any sort of political activity, as their constitutional position demands complete impartiality.

The Court of Session

The judges here are called Senators of the College of Justice, or Lords of Council and Session. They are divided, according to seniority, into the Inner House of eight judges, and the Outer House. The Inner House is subdivided into the First Division chaired by the Lord President of the Court of Session, and the Second Division headed by the Lord Justice-Clerk. The Lord President of the Court of Session and the Lord Justice-General of the High Court are the same person. So are the Lord Justice-Clerk in the High Court and in the Court of Session. The other Court of Session judges are also the Lords Commissioners of Justiciary in the High Court.

The Sheriff Court

The judge here is called the Sheriff, an office dating at least as far back as the twelfth century. The Sheriff must either have been a solicitor or advocate for ten years before his appointment. Sheriffs are appointed by the Sovereign on the recommendation of the Secretary of State for Scotland. If they prove unfit for office, they can be removed only by the Secretary of State through parliament. They must retire at seventy-two. The Sheriff performs many administrative functions in addition to his judicial role.

In civil cases there is an appeal from the Sheriff to the Sheriff Principal. There is a Sheriff Principal for each Sheriffdom (not for each Sheriff Court District). They are full-time judges, although the number of cases referred to them for appeal is fairly small, as appeals can go from the Sheriff directly to the Court of Session. Sheriffs Principal are appointed from senior members of the Scottish Bar, and retire at seventy-two. The Sheriff Principal may appoint Honorary

Sheriffs, who need not have legal qualifications, to hear less important cases thus relieving the load of the full-time Sheriffs.

The District Court

Here ordinary citizens sit on the Bench. They usually have no legal qualifications, but are Justices of the Peace (J.P.s). They are appointed by the Secretary of State for Scotland. The District or Islands Councils have the power to appoint Stipendiary Magistrates to sit in the District Court. They must be advocates or solicitors who have been qualified for at least five years, and they have the powers of a Sheriff. City of Glasgow District Council have made use of this power.

The Legal Profession

Solicitors

The Scottish legal profession is divided into two branches —solicitors and advocates. Solicitors are the people we think of as lawyers. They number approximately 3,500, and they may be in business on their own account, partners in a firm, or individuals employed by a firm. A number of solicitors are employed in local and central government, nationalised industries, or companies, but most are in private practice.

The type of work undertaken by solicitors is enormously varied, although nowadays, particularly in the larger city firms, solicitors often specialise in one or more areas of legal practice. A major area is the field of conveyancing. The layman can attempt to do his own conveyancing, but, in view of the risks involved, it is inadvisable and very uncommon. Unless you choose to do it yourself, only a solicitor can act as your agent in the conveying of heritable property (land and buildings). Solicitors become involved in many other fields. They often take on the role of general professional advisers to clients, managing their investments, completing their tax returns, preparing accounts for small businesses or annual returns for company clients, and so on. Other functions carried out by solicitors are court work, trusts and executries. They undertake much of the litigation in the

Sheriff Courts and District Courts, but they cannot appear in the supreme courts—the High Court of Justiciary, the Court of Session and the House of Lords. Only advocates can appear in these courts, and they are briefed by solicitors to appear on behalf of clients. Individuals cannot instruct an advocate except through a solicitor.

Every practising solicitor in Scotland must be a member of the Law Society of Scotland, which was set up by the Solicitors (Scotland) Act 1949. The Law Society controls the admission of solicitors, regulates professional conduct, handles complaints against its members, and, where necessary, disciplines members. Part of its statutory function is to maintain the Scottish Solicitors' Guarantee Fund, which compensates persons who suffer financial loss as a result of dishonesty on the part of their solicitor. The Law Society also administers the Legal Aid Fund, which, with Treasury grants, finances the system of legal aid in civil and criminal cases, and the Legal Advice and Assistance Scheme. The Society is run by practising solicitors with the aid of a full-time administrative staff. Its headquarters are at Law Society's Hall, Drumsheugh Gardens, Edinburgh. They will advise on solicitors' fees.

There are, in addition, various local societies of solicitors. You will notice, particularly if you live in Edinburgh, that many solicitors' firms have after their names the initials 'W.S.' or 'S.S.C.' The 'W.S.' refers to the Society of Writers to Her Majesty's Signet in Scotland, a society of solicitors with approximately 700 members, based in Edinburgh. The Society of Solicitors in the Supreme Courts of Scotland (S.S.C.) is a similar body, although considerably smaller than the W.S. Society.

Advocates

There are approximately 130 practising advocates (sometimes called 'counsel') in Scotland. Collectively they are known as the Scottish Bar. Only advocates can draft Writs and appear in the supreme courts. They are also entitled to appear in all the lower courts, but they are entirely reliant on solicitors for instructions to act in any case. In addition to their role as pleaders in court, they frequently give written opinions on difficult points of law referred to them by solicitors, and take on a considerable amount of work in tribunals or enquiries (e.g. planning enquiries).

Every advocate is a member of the governing body, the Faculty of Advocates, which has as its elected head the Dean of the Faculty. He has power of discipline over members in professional matters. In addition to being members of Faculty, advocates are Officers of the Court. As such, they have a duty to the court as well as to the clients on whose behalf they appear. This is why they cannot be instructed directly by the client, and why they must be in independent practice and not in any form of partnership.

Highly experienced advocates may be appointed by the Queen to be Queen's Counsel (sometimes called 'Senior Counsel' or 'Q.C.'). The process of becoming a Q.C. is called 'taking silk', as Queen's Counsel wear silk gowns in court. Other advocates are called 'Junior Counsel'.

The Police

The police are the instrument of law and law enforcement most commonly encountered by the individual.

The police service in Scotland is organised to coincide geographically with Regional Council boundaries, with the exception of Lothian and Borders Police (which covers two regions) and Northern Constabulary (which covers Highland Region and the Island Authorities). The police forces in Scotland are:

Central Scotland Police
Dumfries and Galloway Constabulary
Fife Constabulary
Grampian Police
Lothian and Borders Police
Northern Constabulary
Strathclyde Police
Tayside Police

The police force is financed by the Regional Councils and a 50 per cent grant from central government. The Regional Council is responsible for the provision of buildings, equipment and vehicles. Each police force is headed by the Chief Constable, and the Regional Council controls the appointments of the Chief Constable and the Deputy and Assistant Chief Constables, although these appointments are subject to the approval of the Secretary of State for Scotland. The police authority for each force is called the Police Board—a body which exercises responsibility on behalf of the council for the various aspects of the police force under local authority control.

Individual police officers are subject to their Chief Constables for the manner in which they perform their duties, and for any complaint made against them. They are not, strictly speaking, answerable to the Secretary of State for Scotland for their conduct, although central government has a duty to exercise oversight of all aspects of law and order, including the police forces, through the office of the Secretary of State.

In the investigation of crime, the police work in co-operation with the Procurator Fiscal, whose position is, as we have seen, quite independent from the police force. As the person responsible to the Lord Advocate for prosecuting certain offences, the Fiscal has a right to require certain action of, or information from, the police; to that extent only, the police are under his control.

Sheriff Clerks

The administrative machinery of the Sheriff Courts is provided by the Sheriff Clerk, who sits at the desk in front of the Sheriff in court. In cities, the Sheriff Clerk's office can be very large, with different departments dealing with the various sorts of cases—criminal, civil, summary causes, and so on. It is to the Sheriff Clerk that convicted persons should pay fines. Letters pleading guilty to criminal offences, or admitting a debt but asking to be allowed to pay by instalments, should also be sent to the Sheriff Clerk.

Sheriff Officers and Messengers-At-Arms

Sheriff Officers are officers of the Sheriff Court, appointed by the Sheriff Principal for the Sheriffdoms in which they act. There are just over one hundred Sheriff Officers, and they are often organised into partnerships. Their principal function is to enforce decrees of the Sheriff Court—in particular, decrees authorising eviction from rented property and decrees in actions of debt. In the final chapter of this book we examine the role of the Sheriff Officer in the recovery of debts after a court decree (see pp. 144–6).

The equivalent of Sheriff Officers in the Court of Session are Messengers-At-Arms, appointed by the Lord Lyon King of Arms. They enforce decrees of the Court of Session. A large proportion of Sheriff Officers are also Messengers-At-Arms.

THE FAMILY

Marriage

Prior to the Reformation of 1560 much of the law on this subject was Canon or church law, then until 1830 the Commissary Court became the major influence. The influence of both the Pope and the Commissaries was considerable in shaping the law on marriage. When Papal authority ceased in 1540 the vacuum was filled by the Commissaries who were men appointed by the Faculty of Advocates and whose jurisdiction in these matters was more or less exclusive. As one can imagine, wielding such strong control, these men were sometimes unscrupulous, and bribery and corruption were not unknown. In marriage the role of the husband was predominant and the position of the wife would today keep liberationists active for years on end. From 1830 onwards, however, there was a gradual emancipation of the woman and this was reflected in the laws governing this ancient institution. The law of marriage is nowadays contained mainly in the Marriage (Scotland) Act 1977 which came into force on 1st January 1978, replacing a long and sometimes confusing collection of statutes, and introducing several major reforms, principally in relation to marriage procedure.

Engagement

The minimum age for marriage is sixteen, irrespective of sex. As the Act which stipulated this did not mention engagement it is fair to say that boys above the age of fourteen and girls above the age of twelve can enter into such an agreement or contract. Few people would regard their romantic proposal and acceptance as forming a contract but that is what it amounts to.

The contract of engagement may be terminated by agreement between the parties, in which case gifts made to each other should be returned unless they were made irrevocably. If one party refuses to go through with the marriage against the other party's wishes an action of damages for hurt feelings and financial loss is a possible remedy. Understandably, such actions are not common.

Views differ on what should be done with the engagement ring when an engagement is broken off: some hold that it has been given irrevocably, meaning that it need not ever be returned; others take the view that it is conditional upon the marriage taking place and therefore returnable should the marriage not occur. A general principle might be that if the man breaks off the engagement without any justification the woman may keep the ring, but if he has any justification he may recover it. On the other hand if the woman breaks off the engagement without justification she must return it, but not so if she has justification.

Where the engagement is broken off, wedding presents given by third parties are returnable.

The Constitution of Marriage

The law favours succinct phrases and here the phrase is 'the essence of marriage is consent': no consent no marriage. For the state of marriage to come about the parties must both freely and validly exchange their consent, and this consent must be freely given by a man and woman both of whom have the necessary legal capacity, and it must be directed towards a union which is lawful. The consent must also be given in a manner which conforms to the forms prescribed by law. The meaning of these phrases will become clearer in the sections which follow.

Age

The Marriage (Scotland) Act 1977 states that no person domiciled in Scotland may marry before he or she attains the age of sixteen. Parental consent is not necessary in Scotland for persons marrying under the age of eighteen (the age of majority).

Prohibited Degrees of Relationship

The Marriage Act of 1576 legalised all marriages not

prohibited by the Book of Leviticus, chapter 18, and, incredible as it may seem, this was where one had to look for the law before the new Act came into force. There is now a list of relations whom you are not permitted to marry:

1 Mother or Father, Grandmother or Grandfather, Great-grandmother or Great-grandfather.
2 Daughter or Son, Grand-daughter or Grandson, Great-grand-daughter or Great-grandson.
3 Sister or Brother, Nephew or Niece.
4 Aunt or Uncle.
5 Mother's or Grandmother's former husband, Father's or Grandfather's former wife.
6 Mother or Father, Grandmother or Grandfather, of former wife or husband.
7 Daughter or Son, Grand-daughter or Grandson, of former wife or husband.
8 Daughter's or Grand-daughter's former husband, Son's or Grandson's former wife.
9 Adoptive or former adoptive Mother or Father.
10 Adopted or former adopted Daughter or Son.

With the exceptions of 9 and 10, it makes no difference that any person through whom or to whom the relationship is traced is illegitimate. The 'marriage' is still void.

The Formalities

The law concerning the formalities of marriage is the law of the country in which the marriage is performed. Different rules will apply if you decide to get married in deepest South America, but that does not mean to say that the marriage will not be recognised in Scotland.

The Scots law on marriage was regularised by Canon law, and until fairly recently all that was required was acceptance by both parties of each other. As time developed, however, a marriage ceremony would be celebrated after the publication of banns, and this led to the distinction being drawn between regular and irregular marriages. Again, the 1977 Act has brought important changes.

Regular Marriage

Notice

Everyone intending to marry in Scotland must give notice to the District Registrar for the registration district in which the marriage is to take place. The notice must be accompanied by the prescribed fee and the birth certificates of the parties. If either party has been divorced, a copy of the decree of divorce (your solicitor will have obtained this for you after the divorce) must also be produced, and if either party is a widow or widower, the death certificate of the former husband or wife must be presented with the notice. The Registrar displays in his office a list of persons who have given notice, and the proposed dates of the marriages. He also makes an entry in his Marriage Notice Book. This is open for inspection, free of charge, by anyone claiming to object to an intended marriage.

An Objection to Marriage

An objection to a mis-description or inaccuracy in the marriage notice can be corrected by the District Registrar with the approval of the Registrar-General.

If the objection claims there is an alleged impediment to marriage, the Registrar-General must be informed. He will investigate the objection and either advise the District Registrar that there is no legal impediment after all or direct the Registrar to take all reasonable steps to ensure that the marriage does not take place. Meanwhile the Marriage Schedule, allowing the parties to marry, will not be issued. In the case of a religious marriage, if the objection has been received after the issue of the Marriage Schedule the celebrant (the minister or priest) will be advised not to conduct the marriage ceremony.

Legal Impediments

There is a 'legal impediment' to marriage where:

(a) The parties are within the prohibited degrees of relationship listed above (p. 29).

(b) Either of the parties is already married.

(c) Either of the parties will be under sixteen on the date of the intended marriage.

(d) Either of the parties is incapable of understanding the

nature of a marriage ceremony or of consenting to marriage. This is intended, in particular, to cover insanity. If someone objects to the marriage on grounds of incapacity he must produce a medical certificate from a doctor.

(e) Both parties are of the same sex.

(f) Either of the parties is not domiciled in Scotland, and according to the law of the country of domicile there is some ground which would render the marriage void.

Marriage Schedule

Once satisfied that there is no legal impediment, the District Registrar issues a Marriage Schedule. This will not normally be issued less than fourteen days after receipt of the marriage notice, unless one of the parties requests that it be issued earlier. The reasons for the request must be stated and the Registrar-General must authorise it. The Marriage Schedule will also not normally be issued less than seven days before the date of the marriage, so the notice should be given to the District Registrar a good three weeks before the date of the marriage. The Schedule allows the marriage ceremony to go ahead.

The Marriage

In Scotland there are two types of regular marriage—religious and civil. The procedure in both is the same up to the issue of the Marriage Schedule. From this point onwards it is necessary to consider the two separately. A wedding ring, though customary, is not necessary for the validity of a marriage.

Religious Marriage

Under the former law only ministers, clergymen, pastors or priests of religious bodies which were Christian or Jewish could perform religious marriage ceremonies in Scotland. As a result of the 1977 Act the Registrar-General will be able to recognise persons nominated by other religious bodies or sects as being entitled to celebrate religious marriages.

Banns

From 1st January 1978 proclamation of banns by a Church of Scotland minister ceased to be a legally recognised way of giving notice of a marriage; the notice to the District Registrar is now required by law.

The Ceremony

A religious marriage ceremony ('solemnisation of the marriage') cannot take place without a Marriage Schedule. Both parties must be present and there must be two witnesses aged sixteen or over. Immediately after the marriage the parties, the witnesses, and the minister or priest must all sign the Marriage Schedule. The Schedule must be posted or delivered within three days to the District Registrar, who will then enter the marriage in his Register of Marriages.

Civil Marriage

In civil marriages the District Registrar retains the Marriage Schedule. A religious marriage can take place anywhere, but a civil marriage must generally be solemnised in the Registrar's office. He may conduct the marriage elsewhere in his registration district if satisfied that either of the parties is unable to attend his office due to, say, serious illness or bodily injury. In such a case the parties must apply to the Registrar, giving the reasons why one of them cannot attend a registration office. The Registrar will not solemnise a marriage without the Marriage Schedule. The fee for the marriage must be paid, and both parties and two witnesses aged sixteen or over must be present. Immediately after the ceremony the parties, witnesses and Registrar all sign the Marriage Schedule. The Registrar then enters the marriage in his Register of Marriages.

The Grounds of Nullity

A marriage is void if:

(a) either of the parties was under sixteen at the time of the marriage; *or*

(b) the parties are within the prohibited degrees of relationship; *or*

(c) the Marriage Schedule was not given to the minister or priest before the ceremony (this applies to religious marriages); *or*

(d) either party has, by threat, forced the other into marriage; *or*

(e) the consent of one of the parties has been obtained by fraud; *or*

(f) either party went through the marriage ceremony without knowing that it was a marriage; *or*

(g) either party was under error as to the identity of the other party. In this case it would probably be necessary to prove that the marriage would not have gone ahead if the error in identity had been known, and the marriage could be validated by the couple's continuing to cohabit as man and wife after discovering the error.

Anyone can at any time challenge a purported marriage as being void. A void marriage legally never took place, and any children of the union are illegitimate.

In addition to marriages which are void from the outset, some marriages are said to be voidable, that is, either of the parties, but nobody else, can at a later stage have the marriage set aside by the court if he or she raises the appropriate action. The most important example of a marriage which is voidable is where *at the time of the marriage* one of the parties was, unknown to the other party, incurably impotent, that is, permanently incapable of having sexual intercourse. The important difference between void and voidable marriages is that, in voidable marriages, children of the union are legitimate, even though the marriage is annulled. This may seem a strange proposition when considering incurable impotency, but a child born when his parents were unmarried, is legitimated by their subsequent marriage. Thus, an illegitimate child, conceived when both parties were potent, would be legitimated if his parents thereafter married, and, if the marriage was later annulled because, by the time of the marriage, one of the parties was impotent, the earlier-born child would still be legitimate, as the marriage was voidable and not void.

Irregular Marriage

Scots law has given recognition, in exceptional circumstances, to certain types of irregular marriage. At one time there were three possible forms:

1 By declaration between both parties either verbal or written.
2 By the promise of marriage, followed by sexual intercourse consented to on the basis of that promise.
3 Marriage by cohabitation and repute.

Of these forms, only the last is still possible. If the couple live together openly and constantly as husband and wife, so as to cause people to think that they are married, they will be presumed to have exchanged the necessary consent and will be regarded as married. The couple must cohabit 'by bed and board' in Scotland and both parties must be free to marry. No minimum period of cohabitation is laid down, but it must be sufficiently long to give grounds to the belief that they are man and wife. Very few people nowadays seek to establish a marriage by this method.

The Implications of Marriage

For the woman, the most immediate change is the change in her name. By modern custom she usually takes the title 'Mrs' and substitutes her husband's surname for her own. She need not do this and it is becoming quite common for a married woman to retain her maiden name.

In Genesis chapter 3, verse 16, the Lord says to Eve, 'Thy desire shall be towards thy husband and he shall rule over thee.' This view was prevalent in Scotland, but happily the position has now altered, although for many it has not altered enough. A wife is no longer under her husband's curatory (care and control) as previously was so unless she is in minority (between twelve and eighteen). The husband has no power over his wife's conduct nor is it a crime for her to disobey him.

Marriage has legal consequences for the children of the union. A child will be legitimate at birth if his parents were married to each other at the time of his birth. Previously there were considerable differences between the rights of legitimate and illegitimate children, but today there is little distinction between these rights, and illegitimacy is no longer the disadvantage it used to be.

Until very recently, the domicile of the wife upon marriage

became the same as that of her husband. Domicile is not a word which is used frequently, but it has important legal implications. It is something akin to residence but the two are distinct legally. A wife taking her husband's domicile could lead to anomalies in that, if the parties separated, the wife still retained her husband's domicile even though she was, perhaps, living in a separate country. For example, if a Scottish woman married an Australian she was regarded as being domiciled in Australia and would have been unable to obtain a divorce in the Scottish courts. As this could affect jurisdiction in a possible action of divorce, succession and property law, it can easily be seen how unfairly it could operate against the wife.

The Domicile and Matrimonial Proceedings Act 1973 has changed this position. A married woman can now have a domicile independently of her husband and does not automatically have to change her domicile to that of her husband. This is a rule particularly welcome to spouses who are separated, and it illustrates the trend towards emancipation of the woman in marriage.

Duties to Each Other

The spouses should adhere to each other and cohabit together at bed and board, but the husband may choose where the home will be and his wife must accompany him there, provided the place is reasonably suitable in the circumstances. If the title to the house or the lease is in the husband's name only, he has the right to evict the wife. Wives have a similar right if the house or lease is in their name only.

The husband is bound to maintain his wife and provide her with necessary food, clothing and accommodation so long as the marriage endures. Maintaining her in the family home with him is usually sufficient. However, this obligation continues even if she has committed adultery, or been put out of the house, or has reasonable grounds for living apart from her husband.

Marriage is based upon trust and fidelity. For most people difficulties do not arise as to rights, obligations and distribution of assets—these arise when trust is lost. While assuming that normally trust is maintained, we shall summarise some of the items which can lead to difficulties and disagreements in the marriage. Divorce is not a possibility which should be at the forefront of one's mind, but if more people were aware of the problems which can arise at the outset this might cause less heartbreak and unpleasantness later on.

1   Wife's Earnings

These are her own absolute property. She must maintain her husband if he is idle or indigent, but in other circumstances there is no legal duty on her to maintain the common family home.

If the spouses pool the whole or part of their income they will acquire a joint right of property in it irrespective of the amount each may have contributed. A joint bank account does not necessarily mean joint property, but you should consider the possible implications before pooling your income and using only the one account. If both spouses contribute to buying a house, in all likelihood the house will be regarded as joint property and each will be entitled to a one-half share of the proceeds on sale. If you do not want the position to be like that and you each contribute towards the price, you should instruct your lawyer to take the title to the house in your joint names, but showing the split-up of the price.

2   Insurance Policies

You may take out a life insurance policy on the life of your wife or husband. On that person's death you will be entitled to payment of the proceeds.

3   Wife as Husband's Agent

The wife may act as her husband's agent and make him liable for contracts concluded by her either on his express authority or where it can reasonably be implied that she has such authority. In addition, the wife is presumed to have the authority to act as her husband's agent in all matters of household administration normally entrusted to a wife. This extends only to contracts for household necessaries, so husbands need not fear greatly.

4   Housekeeping Allowance

Where the husband allows the wife a periodical lump sum

for housekeeping and similar expenses, she administers this as his agent and has no right, unless authorised, to keep the balance for herself. Few husbands would grudge their wife the right to keep any balance left over from housekeeping, but when there is a conflict the law does not take that view.

5 Furniture in the House

The position regarding furniture is extremely complex and, in the event of a dispute, the court's decision will depend on who bought it, who brought it into the home, whose money paid for it, and by whom it is exclusively used. There is no presumption that you both own the furniture if only one buys it. Articles such as wedding presents will normally be regarded as owned jointly.

6 Gifts Between Husband and Wife

Formerly according to common law you were able to take back any present which you might have given to the other spouse. Such gifts are now, however, irrevocable, which means that any present you receive you may keep.

7 Rights on Death

On the death of one of the spouses the survivor acquires certain rights in that person's estate. These rights are explained in a chapter on Wills, pages 68–9.

Violence in Marriage

Interdict

The principal remedy available to a battered wife is an interdict—a court order prohibiting her husband from coming near her. If the husband breaches the order, he can be brought before the court and fined, or even imprisoned, if the action is in the Court of Session (e.g. if the interdict is included in a divorce action which has been started). If it is a Sheriff Court action of interdict, a further action for breach may be brought, and the husband fined or imprisoned. Imprisonment for breach of interdict is, however, extremely rare.

It is also possible to obtain 'interim interdict', which is a temporary order to protect the wife until the application for interdict can be decided. An interim interdict can be obtained very quickly indeed.

Lawburrows

One of the difficulties in cases of domestic violence is that most assaults do not take place in front of witnesses and, therefore, an action of interdict may not be possible. The action of lawburrows, however, requires only one witness (in general, Scots law requires at least two independent witnesses), and that witness can be the wife herself. It is an action which is not commonly used, partly due to the fact that its application to cases of domestic violence has only recently been realised, and, as it has been only rarely used, very few solicitors know anything about it.

In an action of lawburrows, the person complained against has to lodge a sum of money with the court (called 'caution') which he forfeits if he continues to molest the pursuer. It is available where a wife fears for her safety or for the safety of her children or property.

The action of lawburrows is cheaper than interdict, but its main disadvantages are: firstly, that there is no interim remedy so that, until the case is heard, the violent husband is under no constraint; secondly, that the husband is not forbidden from coming near his wife—he merely has to refrain from threats or violence.

The Police

The police are very reluctant to interfere in domestic disputes, largely because there are usually no witnesses, and there will not be sufficient evidence to enable them to charge the husband. If, however, you have obtained interdict or interim interdict, you should let the police see a copy of the court order, and they will, in such circumstances, be more willing to help you.

Further Information

Scottish Women's Aid have produced an excellent booklet entitled *Battered Women in Scotland: Your Rights and Where To Turn for Help*, which is available from Scottish Women's Aid, 11 St Colme Street, Edinburgh, and from Citizen's Advice Bureaux.

Children

Legitimate Children

A legitimate child is a child either conceived or born in lawful marriage or a child born in a marriage (called 'putative') which proves to be voidable (see p. 33). A child born to a married woman is presumed to be her husband's, provided it is born sufficiently after the marriage. A child born in adultery or casual cohabitation is not legitimate. A child is also 'legitimated' if, at some time following his birth, his parents marry.

Registration of the Birth

A parent or parents or any relative who knows of the birth, or any person present at the birth, must attend personally at the Registrar's office within twenty-one days to give statutory particulars of the birth. An extract birth certificate will then be issued.

Illegitimate Children

An illegitimate child is a child born to a woman who, at the time of its conception or its birth or at any time between, was not validly married to the father of that child. Previously, according to common law, a bastard child was entitled to none of the rights conferred upon legitimate children, but this position has now largely been altered.

Registration of the Birth

The birth must be registered in the same way as a legitimate child, but the Registrar may not register on information supplied by the father alone, nor may he enter the name of any person as father unless at both parents' request.

The mother must produce a declaration stating that a particular person is the father and a statutory declaration by him acknowledging himself to be the father. If no mention of the parent is desired it is possible to obtain an abbreviated birth certificate.

Aliment

If paternity is not established the mother must bear the whole expense of maintaining the child. If it is established then both parents will be liable to contribute. If Social Security is provided, the Department of Health and Social Security may bring an action against the father seeking a contribution towards the maintenance.

Parental Rights and Obligations

Parental rights and powers can be divided into two kinds: those of guidance and those of legal administration. Both parents have the right of custody and the power to regulate the child's upbringing while the child is a pupil (under fourteen for boys and under twelve for girls). This power continues, gradually diminishing, until the child passes from the age of minority into majority at eighteen.

Custody

Both parents have the right of custody of the child. Previously only the father had this right, but this position has changed, although in a situation of conflict the parent who has had possession of the child will often be in a stronger position. In all questions concerning custody, the welfare of the child is of paramount importance. This means considering his health, happiness, the accommodation in the home and the education facilities. The court also considers the suitability of each of the parties as a parent. Unless she is clearly unsuitable, the mother will be preferred in most cases, but it is becoming more common for a father to succeed in obtaining custody. A father is obliged to maintain his child from want until the child can maintain himself by his own efforts. If the father is dead, the child may claim aliment from his relatives in the following order: 1 Mother. 2 Grandparents. 3 Higher ascendants, e.g. Great-grandparents.

Education

Parents must provide education for their children, normally by ensuring attendance at a local authority or other school between the ages of five and sixteen. Local authorities operate a system of catchment areas which determines what school children from any particular area should go to. In practice it is very difficult to persuade the local education authority to allow a child to attend a school outside the catchment area unless, of course, the parents are prepared to send their child to a fee-paying school. If the child fails to attend regularly the parents are liable to be prosecuted.

Contractual Rights of Children

The role of the family in everyday life might seem relatively simple but a major part of it will be governed by the law of contract. Before one can discuss contract law one must first consider the question of 'legal personality'. Legal personality enables an individual to undertake and be bound by legal obligations—unless you are a legal person you will not be able to draw the benefits of a legal system, such as enforcing your rights under contracts and raising court actions. Legal personality is not only given to individuals but also to companies. A company as large as Shell Oil will be considered a single legal entity even though it is made up of several thousand individuals.

Generally speaking, legal personality in an individual can be said to begin at conception and end at death.

1 Unborn Child

The unborn child has legal personality to a very limited extent only. If the unborn child is subsequently born alive an action may be brought on his behalf, for example, for compensation for ante-natal injuries, but should the child be still-born he will legally never have existed.

2 Pupils

This does not refer to school children but rather to children who, because of their age, are not attributed full legal personality, but are in the 'guidance and control' of their 'tutor', their parent or some other administrator. Pupils are boys under fourteen and girls under twelve.

A pupil has no capacity to contract by himself and any contract must be entered into by his tutor on his behalf. The tutor will usually be one of the child's parents. A pupil cannot sue or be sued on his own account—the tutor must act for him. A pupil can own a house, but he has not the capacity to make a Will.

3   Minors

This is the stage beyond pupillarity. The age is fourteen for boys and twelve for girls. Minors have legal personality and may enter contracts either with or without the consent of an advisor, who is in this case called a 'curator'—again usually a parent. With a few qualifications, a minor can bind himself to any personal obligations, engage in a trade, or become a shareholder in a company. There is a safeguard for the minor who enters into contracts. His contracts are 'voidable' or open to cancellation at any time during the four years after he has attained majority, if he can show that the other party to the contract took advantage of his age. This is not an open-ended let-out, but where a substantial loss can be shown then the law will act to protect the minor.

A minor can sue and be sued, but when he is being sued his curator must be called with him as a defender. He may purchase and sell property and he may even be declared bankrupt! Minority ends for both boys and girls at the age of eighteen (it used to be twenty-one). From then he or she must face the full obligations and responsibilities of the legal system—subject, of course, to the four-year period mentioned above.

We have already pointed out the importance of age in marriage. In Scotland a marriage is only valid if both parties are sixteen and no parental consent is required for persons who marry under eighteen.

Tutors and Curators

According to common law the father was always the tutor or curator, but now both parents have equal rights and it is quite open for the mother to be in one or both of these positions. One becomes a tutor or curator by virtue of parenthood and no application to the court is required to confirm it. While the terminology might be confusing, the roles are, generally speaking, simple and if you are in doubt your solicitor or your local Citizens' Advice Bureau will advise you on your duties to your children.

The local authority has the power to take into their care any child who has neither parent nor guardian, or who, for some reason, is not being properly maintained to the extent that such intervention is necessary for the welfare of that child. For further information we recommend *Women's Rights: a Practical Guide* by Anna Coote and Tess Gill, page 461 (Penguin, 2nd edition 1977).

Adoption

The law on adoption is at present in the middle of change. The Children Act 1975, which is being brought into force gradually, will eventually radically alter the procedure of adoption, but at the time of writing many of the important innovations made by the Act have still not been implemented.

Only persons who are at least twenty-one years old can adopt a child. In most cases, adoption is by married couples and the application will be made by them jointly. A married person cannot apply alone unless his or her spouse cannot be found, or the couple are separated and the separation seems likely to be permanent, or the wife or husband is incapable, due to physical or mental illness, of applying for adoption. An unmarried person can apply to adopt a child, but an unmarried man is unlikely to succeed in an application to adopt a young female child.

It is fairly common for a parent to apply to adopt his or her child if the parents are divorced and the parent who has custody of the child has remarried. If the wife has obtained custody and the husband is required to pay money to maintain the child or children, he will be entitled to tax relief on these payments. If, however, he gives his ex-wife nothing towards the upbringing of the children, she may find on remarriage that her second husband is bearing the cost of maintaining the children of her first marriage without being entitled to any tax relief. One remedy is for the mother and her second husband to seek to adopt the child. A parent may not, however, adopt his or her child without the consent of the other parent. The court must be satisfied that the other parent agrees unconditionally to the adoption of the child, and knows exactly the effect of giving consent in terms of loss of parental rights. In certain circumstances, the consent can be dispensed with if the parent cannot be found, in spite of all reasonable steps having been taken to trace him or her, or is dead, or is incapable of giving consent, or is unreasonably withholding agreement, or has abandoned, neglected or ill-treated the child.

A mother cannot consent to the adoption of her child until the child is at least six weeks old.

In addition to provisions regarding parental consent, the child, if a minor (i.e. a girl aged twelve or over or a boy aged fourteen or over) must also consent to being adopted, although again this may be dispensed with if the court is satisfied that the child is incapable of giving consent.

Only children under the age of eighteen can be adopted, and if a child is or has ever been married, he or she cannot be adopted.

Procedure

The procedure for adoption will be changed in several important respects when the Children Act 1975 is in full force. At present a petition is presented to the Court of Session, or, more usually, the Sheriff Court, together with the birth certificate of the child, and, if the applicants are married, their marriage certificate. A medical certificate as to the health of each of the applicants must also be obtained unless one of them is the child's parent. The child must have been living with the applicants for the previous three months, and the petition states the date on which the child was received into the care of the applicants.

When the petition has been presented, the court appoints a *curator ad litem*, who is often a local solicitor. He or she visits the house and reports back to the court on, among other things, the accommodation and general living conditions, the means of the applicants, the welfare of the child, and other general information required for the petition.

If neither of the applicants is a parent of the child, three months' notice of intention to apply to adopt the child must also be given to the local authority. Any other relevant consent forms must also be obtained from the local authority.

A court hearing is not usually necessary, but the court can refuse to grant the petition until the applicants or the child are interviewed in court. Any proceedings in the court are held *in camera*, which means that the public and the press are excluded, and the various papers relating to the application are also confidential.

In coming to a decision, the court's first concern is the welfare of the child, and the child's own wishes are ascertained. The effect of an adoption order is to extinguish the parental rights of the child's natural parents or guardian and to transfer these rights and duties to the adoptive parents. It also ends the liability of the natural parents to maintain the child. The child is treated in all respects as the legitimate child of the adoptive parents, and acquires rights in the estates of the adoptive parents when they die. The corollary of this is that the child loses rights in the estates of his or her natural parents (unless they died after 10th September 1964 *and* the adopters died before that date). The child also takes the surname of the adopter or adopters.

The Registrar-General for Scotland maintains an Adopted Children Register, with details of the child and of the adoption order. An adopted child has a right, on reaching the age of seventeen, to see particulars of his or her birth.

Further Information

Association of British Adoption and Fostering Agencies
Scottish Secretary
28 West Craigs Crescent
Edinburgh EH12 8NB
031–334 1547

Criminal Offences by Children

The age of criminal responsibility in Scotland is eight, and a child under that age cannot be guilty of any offence. There are also special provisions for the prosecution of offenders under the age of sixteen, who are generally dealt with by Children's Panels, rather than in the ordinary courts.

Children's Panels

These were set up under the Social Work (Scotland) Act 1968 to deal with offences by children under sixteen. Each local authority district maintains a panel of volunteers, on whose services the Reporter, a full-time Regional Authority officer, can call. The panel for each case (called a 'children's hearing') comprises three lay persons, including one member of each sex. The initial investigation of an offence is made by the Reporter, who decides whether or not to refer the case to a hearing. If he refers a case, he gives a statement of his reasons for doing so, and calls for reports from the Social Work Department. The child's parents have a right to attend the hearing—indeed, they may be required to do so—and the child can also be accompanied by a representative, who need not be legally qualified.

At the hearing, from which the public are excluded, the members of the panel discuss the case with the child, his parents and representatives, if present, and consider the report from the Social Work Department and any other reports. If the child admits the offence, the Children's Panel can order a supervision requirement (the equivalent of what we used to call 'probation') or place the child in a residential establishment (what we used to call an 'approved school'). The panel can also, at its discretion, decide that no punishment should be given. It has no power to fine the child, nor can it impose any penalty on the parents.

If the child denies the offence the case goes to a hearing, in private, before the Sheriff. If he decides that the alleged offence has been proved, he refers the case back to the panel who then proceed in the manner outlined above. It is possible to appeal to the Court of Session against the Sheriff's decision.

Every order of the Children's Panel must be reviewed at least once a year, and the child's parents can demand more frequent reviews. If a supervision requirement is made, it lasts until the child is eighteen, and in the three months before that date the Reporter arranges another hearing to decide whether further supervision is required.

The child, his parents, or the Reporter can appeal from the Children's Panel to the Sheriff Court. There is a further appeal to the Court of Session, but only on a point of law or for an alleged irregularity in the conduct of the case. In other words, the Sheriff's decision on the facts of the case is final.

The procedure outlined above is followed in the large majority of offences by children, but if the crime is a serious one the Lord Advocate may decide that the case should be heard not by a Children's Panel, but in the Sheriff Court or High Court. A child found guilty of murder will be ordered by the High Court to be detained during Her Majesty's Pleasure. In less serious cases, the court can make an order for detention, residential training, or probation, or it may impose a fine, or admonish, or discharge the child. The District Court has no power to hear trials of offenders under the age of sixteen.

Further Information

On health and sex:

Scottish Health Education Unit
21 Lansdowne Crescent
Edinburgh EH12 5EH
031–337 3251/2

Further Reading

Marriage, Divorce and the Family in Scotland, David Nichols—Scottish Association of Citizens' Advice Bureaux (50p)

The Layman's Guide to Scots Law. Volume 2: 'Divorce', Richard M. Keith and George B. Clark—Gordon Bennett Publications (2nd edition 1977) 65p.

Battered Women: Your Rights and Where to Turn for Help, Mrs Margaret A. F. Gimblett and others—Scottish Women's Aid

Women's Rights: A Practical Guide, Anna Coote and Tess Gile—Penguin Books (£1.25)

Where to Get Family Planning Advice—available free of charge from the Scottish Health Education Unit

Sources of Help

Solicitors

Citizens' Advice Bureaux

District Council Social Work Departments

Scottish Women's Aid
11 St Colme Street
Edinburgh
031–225 8011

Further sources of help are given on page 63.

DIVORCE

While divorce is not the tragedy it was, in social terms, only a few years ago, it is still a distressing and regrettably increasingly common occurrence. Scots law has recently undergone major revision of this subject and we shall consider the position as it is today. We cannot, within the pages of this book, offer advice on marriage counselling but we can stress that there are numerous organisations such as the Scottish Marriage Guidance Council who are willing to offer assistance, either by attempting to prevent the final breakdown or by assisting to rebuild the new life.

Jurisdiction

The present law on divorce is contained in the Divorce (Scotland) Act 1976. It is important to realise that this Act affects Scotland only, and as with similar such statutes, before a case can competently be heard in a Scottish court that court must have jurisdiction or the power to hear it. Jurisdiction is an essential aspect of any court case but the way in which it is applied may vary considerably from country to country, and in some countries it is easier to get a divorce than in others.

In Scotland, to enable a Scottish court to hear your divorce case, you must either be 'resident' or 'domiciled' in Scotland. The Court of Session in Edinburgh, which is the only court in Scotland which can hear divorces, has jurisdiction only if one of the parties to the marriage either (a) is domiciled in Scotland, i.e. lives in Scotland and regards Scotland as his or her home, or alternatively lives outside Scotland while still regarding Scotland as his or her home; or (b) has been habitually resident in Scotland for a period of one year immediately preceding the date on which the action of divorce is begun.

If you comply with either or both of these conditions you may proceed with an action of divorce regardless of where your husband or wife, as the case may be, lives. If you do not fall within either category you must wait until you have satisfied at least the residence requirement (*b*) before you can take steps to obtain your divorce.

Jurisdiction is not complicated and parties to a marriage may find they have jurisdiction in both Scotland and England. As the law south of the border differs not only in its statutory aspects but also in its practical procedure it may be worthwhile to consider the relative advantages of both jurisdictions.

The Grounds for Divorce

Formerly divorce by consent was legally impossible and the courts sought to blame one or other of the parties to the marriage. The 1976 Act changed that, and now the only ground for divorce in Scotland is the 'irretrievable breakdown of the marriage'. The Act does not oblige the court to declare that the marriage has broken down, rather it states that the marriage will be held to have broken down if a certain specified set of circumstances can be seen to exist. For simplicity's sake these circumstances can be considered as 'grounds'. They are:

1 *Adultery*. That at some point since the date of the marriage the defender (the party against whom the divorce is sought) has committed adultery. The lover (paramour) may or may not be named in the summons. Sometimes it is possible to get expenses from the lover. The action will not be successful if the adultery has been 'connived at' or 'condoned' by the pursuer (the party seeking divorce).

To condone the adultery the husband and wife must continue or resume living together as man and wife in the full knowledge of the adultery. Mere sexual intercourse in the knowledge of the adultery is not sufficient to establish condonation.

Connivance can be taken as meaning tacit permission. This would occur prior to the adulterous act: for example, the husband may agree to leave the house in order that the wife can commit adultery with her lover and be suitably caught in the act. The court takes an extremely serious view of any attempt to put up a false case or withhold a justified defence. Until the present Act came into force the pursuer had to take an oath (the Oath of Calumny) to the effect that no such collusion had taken place. The oath has been abolished, as now that divorce by consent is possible there is little that can be gained by collusion and its significance has largely ceased.

2 *Intolerable Conduct.* That at some time since the date of the marriage the defender has behaved in such a way that the pursuer cannot reasonably be expected to live with him or her. It does not matter that the unreasonable conduct may have been unintentional nor that it may have arisen from mental abnormality or some similar disorder. What amounts to intolerable conduct is for the court to decide but it probably includes physical assault, humiliating behaviour, excessive sexual demands or wilful refusal, habitual drunkenness, neglect amounting to abandonment (e.g. the husband obsessed by his work), insanity, and perhaps even imprisonment for a serious criminal offence.

3 *Desertion.* That the defender has wilfully and without reasonable cause deserted the pursuer for a continuous period of two years immediately prior to the commencement of the action. It remains to be seen exactly what interpretation the court will place on the words 'wilfully and without reasonable cause', but desertion will require both actual separation and an intention (wilful) of one spouse to desert the other. The action will not succeed if it can be shown that the pursuer refused a genuine and reasonable offer from the defender to live together once more. Again it is a question of circumstances whether a particular offer to resume married life is considered genuine and reasonable.

4 *Separation and Consent.* That the husband and wife have not lived together (cohabited) for a continuous period of two years immediately prior to the commencement of the court action *and* the defender consents to the granting of the decree of divorce. Both requirements must be met. To show consent the defender has simply to sign a notice of consent attached to the summons and return it to the court within fourteen days. A further notice on the summons makes quite clear to the defender the consequences of consenting. The Act stipulates that nothing must be concealed from the defender, and he or

she has the right to withdraw consent at any time prior to the granting of the decree.

5 *Separation*. That the parties have not lived together for a period of five years prior to the commencement of the action. The consent of the defender is not necessary, but it is not as straightforward as it might seem since the Act gives the court discretion to refuse to grant a divorce if it is of the opinion that 'grave financial hardship' to the defender might result.

You will see from the last ground that the court can refuse to grant a decree of divorce if it is of the opinion that grave financial hardship could result. Just what is grave financial hardship? In all probability the situation will not arise in the case of couples who are married early and seek divorce at an early age. Both will probably be quite capable of earning their own respective livelihoods and, particularly if no children are involved, it is unlikely that financial hardship (greater than might have existed during marriage) will arise. Grave financial hardship does include the loss of the chance of acquiring any benefit, and the loss of pension rights by older women may give the court sufficient ground to establish the possibility of grave financial hardship and thereby refuse to grant the divorce.

Judicial Separation

Divorce is not the only solution to the problem of incompatibility. Separation is the single step away from the final decision and it is possible either with or without the court's approval and knowledge. Informal separation is a perfectly acceptable position provided the parties are able to maintain sufficiently harmonious relations in order to care for the needs of both the respective spouses and any children of the marriage. In the situation where the parties are unable to agree to any peaceful or non-judicial arrangement the Act also applies, and the grounds for a judicial separation are the same as the five situations previously stated. In other words, the same grounds which justify the irretrievable breakdown of the marriage also justify a decree of judicial separation.

In fact, where the parties have already gone before the

court and obtained a judicial separation, the 'extract decree' or judgment granting the separation will, except in the case of adultery, be sufficient proof of the facts when it comes to seeking a divorce. That is to say, the facts on which the earlier action was based probably will not need to be proved again. The pursuer must still appear in court and the earlier granting of the decree of separation will not prevent this. It is interesting to note that in England it is now possible to obtain a postal divorce without either of the parties attending in person.

Reconciliation

Views differ as to how great a part the court, or indeed any institutional body, should play in reconciliation. In our view it is better for the individual to be made aware of the services available rather than to have them thrust upon him. In the Act the court has an obligation to continue the hearing if it is the judge's view that there is a reasonable chance of reconciliation. This means that the divorce action will not be settled one way or the other, but is suspended to see whether reconciliation can be achieved.

The periods of time allowed for reconciliation vary according to whether your action for divorce is based on adultery, desertion or separation. It is simplest to consider each case separately.

1 *Adultery*. In this case the court allows three months during which the couple can live together again without forfeiting their right to a divorce. The three months is a single continuous period which begins from the date when the couple start to live together again. The couple need not live together continuously throughout the three-month period, but if there is any cohabitation after the conclusion of that period then the right to a divorce will be lost. If, for example, a wife, who has separated from her husband because of his adultery, returns and stays with him for a short period—perhaps one week— this will not prevent her from obtaining a subsequent divorce on the grounds of his adultery. If, however, she again decides that she cannot endure living with him in these circumstances and leaves, but later returns after the expiry of the three

months from the time when they first lived together again, she will have forfeited the right to obtain the divorce. The essential point is that three months only are allowed for reconciliation once the parties have resumed married life together.

2 *Desertion or Separation.* This can be subdivided into desertion where:
- (*a*) the parties have been apart for the required two-year separation period;

and desertion or separation where:
- (*b*) the parties have been apart but the two-year period or five-year period has not elapsed.

In (*a*) the Act provides that a similar three-month period is available for reconciliation as with the case of adultery. The same rules and restrictions apply.

In (*b*) a maximum period of six months is allowed for reconciliation both in the separation periods of two and five years. Unlike the three-month period mentioned above, this is not a single continuous period of six months, but it is arrived at by adding together all the separate days, weeks and months during which the parties have cohabited. So long as you do not overstep the six-month limit the periods of two and five years will not be interrupted, but any period during which the couple do cohabit is added to the two or five years. Thus, where a couple have separated and subsequently resumed cohabitation during the two or five years for a period of, say, three months, then the total period of time required to establish desertion or separation is two years and three months or five years and three months.

The provisions regarding reconciliation might seem complicated but in actual fact they are not. Provided one adheres to the time-limits there will be no difficulty in following the rules which have been laid down.

Procedure
The First Meeting

Having made an appointment with a solicitor, you should take your marriage certificate and a birth certificate for each of your children under sixteen years of age. If the originals have been lost copies can be obtained from the Registrar of Births, Deaths and Marriages, Waterloo Place, Edinburgh. At this meeting your solicitor will seek facts and information from you. He will want to know your full name, address and occupation and also that of your spouse. Similarly with your children. He will enquire into your financial situation and determine whether or not you will qualify for legal aid.

The first interview will also cover the history of your marriage. Some of the questions you will be asked will be of a personal nature, but it is important that you answer them correctly as the solicitor has to assess if there is a sufficient case to enable you to proceed with an action for divorce. You may feel uneasy at discussing this with the solicitor as, in many cases, he will probably be a young assistant and much less experienced than yourself in these matters. While you might find this interview embarrassing you should not be afraid to give a full explanation of the facts as, to the solicitor, it will not have the same emotional undertones which make it so difficult for you to retell. This, perhaps, is one instance of the advantage of his objectivity. The solicitor will also ask for details about the provisions which you are able to make for your children. It is very important for the court to be certain that, if you are to get custody of them, you will be able to care for them properly.

When telling the solicitor about your marriage you should also give him the name and address of any helpful witnesses. Your doctor might be able to provide valuable testimony and, if so, his name should be noted.

The witnesses will be required to complete questionnaires sent to them by your solicitor. If he does not send them questionnaires he will ask them to call in to see him, and the statement which he then prepares is called a 'precognition'. The purpose of this is to obtain corroboration of your own story. While many of the events will be known only to yourself, it is useful to have as much of your story corroborated by someone else as is possible.

The Summons

The solicitor then prepares his papers to send to the advocate. The client does not choose the advocate. This is the choice of the solicitor, but whoever is chosen will be able to proceed

without further communication with you. When he receives
the papers the advocate will draft the summons. This is a
formal document which embodies your own and the witnesses' statements and states your case as succinctly as possible. It is divided into three parts and follows a formalised
style. It narrates who the parties are—namely you (the pursuer) and your spouse (the defender). It states the date and
place of the marriage and the dates and places of birth of any
children of the marriage under sixteen years of age. It goes on
to detail the circumstances of the case and any specific
incidents it is founded upon. This part is, in effect, a summary
of the information which you gave your solicitor at the first
interview. The draft summons is sent to the solicitor by the
advocate to be typed up by the solicitor's secretary and then
passed through a court process called 'signetting'. After this a
copy is sent, by recorded delivery, to the defender, but these
are all details which are taken care of by the solicitor. Normally the defender has fourteen days within which to enter
appearance, i.e. to intimate to the court that he will be
defending the action. The vast majority of divorces are not
defended but there is very often something in the summons to
which your husband or wife may object. For example, the
summons may request the court to order your husband to pay
£x per week towards the maintenance of each of your children, whereas he may feel that he can only afford a lesser
amount per week. He may object to your seeking a periodical
allowance for yourself. These are not objections 'on the
merits' of the action, and in most cases agreement is eventually reached and the action will proceed as undefended.
If the defender has such objections his solicitor will still formally enter appearance in order to protect his position in case
the parties are unable to agree. The defender's solicitor will
also enter appearance if your spouse really does intend to
defend the action on its merits, i.e. where he or she disputes
the facts on which the action is based or wishes to contest
questions such as who has custody of the children.

The Undefended Divorce

On 25th April 1978, several important changes were
introduced for undefended divorces. In any action of divorce,
or of separation and aliment, raised on or after 25th April

1978, where the action is undefended or, at a later stage, becomes undefended, evidence may be given by way of sworn statements, called 'affidavits', and it is no longer necessary for you or your witnesses to attend the court to give evidence. The affidavit must be given before a Notary Public (your solicitor, or another solicitor from his firm, will probably be a Notary Public). If the advocate is satisfied that the written statements and supporting documents are satisfactory, he will prepare a document, called a 'Minute', which your solicitor will lodge with the Court of Session. Assuming that the judge is satisfied, he will grant decree in your favour.

The new procedure will cut down on the travelling time and cost incurred in bringing you and your witnesses to the court. You should, however, note that it does not apply in cases where the court considers that the defender is suffering from mental disorder, nor, of course, does it apply to actions which are defended. The court does, however, have the power to apply the new procedure where the merits (i.e. the facts, such as the reasons for the irretrievable breakdown of the marriage) of the action are not disputed, even if the action is defended on an ancillary matter, such as the division of property.

Custody and Maintenance of the Children

Under the new procedure, at least one affidavit must come from an independent party, that is, a person who is neither the husband nor wife in the action, and who can speak for the welfare of each of the children of the marriage under the age of sixteen. This safeguard emphasises the attitude of the court: that, on the divorce of their parents, the welfare of children is of paramount importance.

The Defended Divorce

The vast majority of divorces are undefended but circumstances may arise where your spouse (the defender) is not prepared to accept what has been said in the summons as true. If this happens he or she will defend the action 'on its merits' (meaning that he or she will contest the allegations made in the summons).

The most common grounds for contesting divorces are on the question of custody of children or on the financial aspects.

Hopefully such disputes can be ironed out before the case reaches the stage of a court hearing, but there will be cases where no agreement can be reached, and in this event the only solution is the defended proof.

Both parties will be required to appear in the Court of Session in Edinburgh with their respective witnesses. This means that the services of both an Edinburgh solicitor and an advocate will be required (see p. 23).

If you live outside Edinburgh and have a local solicitor, you will be met at the court by a solicitor who represents the Edinburgh firm who is handling your case. This solicitor will have been briefed by your own local solicitor, so he should be familiar with the circumstances of the case and will be able to assist you as required.

The Court of Session is situated in the High Street in Edinburgh behind St Giles' Cathedral. Divorce cases start at 10 a.m. so you should ensure that you are there in ample time. Either your own or the Edinburgh solicitor will meet you and check that your witnesses have also arrived. He will explain the procedures to you and he will tell you when you can expect your case to be heard. Ideally he should also introduce you to your counsel, the advocate who will be representing you, and he too should calm your nerves by running through the sort of questions which he will be asking you.

When it is your turn to go into the court the judge will stand up and ask you to take the oath. You raise your right hand and swear that, 'the evidence which I shall give shall be the truth, the whole truth and nothing but the truth'. You will then be questioned.

Evidence is led first on behalf of the pursuer and then on behalf of the defender. All witnesses are liable to be cross-examined by the advocate for the other party. This process can be a very distressing one for the parties to the action. At the end of the hearing the judge usually gives his decision, but in some cases he may wish to take time to consider his judgment.

The divorce is effective from the day of the court hearing, but there is a period of twenty-one days during which your husband or wife may appeal. This is highly unlikely, but for this reason you should not remarry during this period. When the time-limit for appeal has passed you will be sent an extract decree of divorce and this document sets out the terms of the divorce.

The costs of a defended divorce will vary considerably and in some instances the expenses may well exceed £1,000. The defended proof will, by its very nature, be an emotional and unpleasant affair, but a large proportion of the work will fall upon the respective solicitors who will endeavour to adjust the written pleadings as much as possible so that when the case comes to court it is only the most burning issues which have to be decided by the judge.

Financial Provisions on Divorce

While all might have been harmony at the time of the marriage as soon as a rift appears goodwill disappears and arguments develop as to who owns what and who paid for what. Numerous complications can arise, and as greed is one of man's common instincts it is not difficult to see that the financial aspect of divorce is one which leads to considerable litigation and personal dispute. The Act has made changes to the law on this subject and the position can be generally stated as follows.

Either party to the marriage, the husband or the wife, may at any time prior to the court granting decree of divorce apply for one or more of the following orders:

1 An order for a periodical allowance, e.g. a weekly allowance paid by the one party to the other.
2 A capital sum.
3 An order for the variation of an ante-nuptial or post-nuptial marriage settlement.

The last point (3) will be relatively uncommon as, in the vast majority of cases, such financial contracts are no longer made before or after the marriage.

No specific mention is made in the Divorce (Scotland) Act 1976 of an order for aliment, i.e. payment of an allowance for the maintenance of children of the marriage. Legislation already exists to provide for this and the relevant provisions have not been repealed by the 1976 Act. At present the law regarding financial provisions is under review and no doubt the position will be changed. For a more detailed explanation of aliment see p. 40.

Before any financial order is granted by the court in a divorce action, consideration will be given to the respective means of both parties and to all the circumstances of the case. We have explained that the solicitor will want to obtain details of salary earnings, general income and expenditure, and it is for this reason that those questions are asked. The court will seek to take an overall picture of the situation and will not prejudice one party to the advantage of the other if by doing so one party would be unfairly handicapped.

It is not obligatory to apply for any of the above orders, and if you do not wish to then you need not do so. The solicitor will advise on this: but this might be a situation where you, the client, should take the driving reins and insist that no further action is taken if you do not wish to inflict further punishment on your spouse. While the solicitor might advise you to obtain further money your own personal view might be that the other party has suffered enough and that the end does not justify the means. If you decide at the time of the divorce that you do not wish to make any of the orders, that decision does not prevent you from later applying to the court for an order for a periodical allowance.

Once an order has been given either party may apply to the court for a variation or alteration of that order—but they must be able to show that there has been a change in circumstances justifying the application. In the event of the death of either of the parties this right is also given to the executor (the administrator of the deceased's estate).

The court controls the financial situation of the parties for some time after the divorce. If there is a substantial change in circumstances, either party may apply to the court for payment of a periodical allowance or for the variation or cessation of such payment.

A capital sum can neither be applied for nor varied after the decree of divorce has been granted.

When Do Such Orders Cease to Have Effect?

Most important under this heading is the order for a periodical allowance. This will cease only when the court varies it or upon the remarriage or death of the person for whose benefit it is paid. This means that should you be found liable to pay such an allowance this liability will not cease on your death but will continue to be payable out of whatever estate you might leave until the death of your spouse. The same applies to aliment for children: on your death it continues to be paid out of your estate. Although the death of a person to whom the allowance is payable brings the order to an end, any arrears of the payment still have to be settled. You can see that if you remarry while still obliged to pay your first wife a periodical allowance your second wife will, in effect, be contributing to maintaining the first wife and any children of that previous marriage. This is a situation of which you should be aware as it can cause considerable stress and anxiety to the parties of the second marriage.

Financial Provisions on Divorce by Separation

In the case of divorce following the separation periods of two or five years, the court will lay down rules to make certain that the pursuer has taken sufficient steps to ensure that the defender is aware of the financial provisions, and also of any provisions regarding an order for the maintenance and custody of the children of the marriage. If the pursuer alleges that the other party's whereabouts or address are unknown to him or her then the court will have to be satisfied that all reasonable steps have been taken to trace an address and to advise the other party accordingly. These provisions ensure that a divorce will not be granted without the other party being made aware of their rights. This is a safeguard which will be rigorously enforced by the court.

Anti-Avoidance Provisions

Financial considerations play such an important part that the Act has to safeguard the position of the spouse in whose favour an award has been made. The rules are complicated but the broad effect is to enable the court to reduce, vary or prohibit settlements or transfers of property made by the defender within certain specified time-limits, and made with a view to defeating the pursuer's claim. Once again it is probably man's instinct to avoid paying money which he does not feel that he deserves to pay. The provisions safeguarding these orders are not new but the Act has widened their scope.

It has also introduced a significant change in that the court may now make an order if it is shown that the transfer was, or is about to be made, 'wholly or partially' for the purpose of defeating the pursuer's financial claim. Previously the court could only interfere if the transfer was shown to be primarily for that purpose.

The law places a significance on words and this is one illustration of that significance. To many people there might not appear to be much difference between these two phrases, but the distinction does give the court wider powers and a greater ability to prevent the deliberate disposal of property.

The anti-avoidance provisions apply if an application has been made for any of the following:

1 (a) An order for the payment of a periodical allowance.
  (b) An order for the payment of a capital sum.
  (c) An order for a periodical allowance or its variation after the date of the divorce.
  (d) An order varying or altering a periodical allowance following a change in the circumstances of either party.
  or
2 An action for separation and aliment, adherence and aliment or interim aliment which has been brought by either party.
  or
3 An application for variation of an award of aliment.

The pursuer can apply for an order to alter or prevent the transfer of property by the defender at any time before the expiry of one year from the date when the application in 1, 2 and 3 above was dealt with. That order, if granted, will take into account any transfer made to any other person during the three-year period prior to making the claim in court. This is complicated and can be illustrated with the following example.

Mrs Z makes an application to the court for payment of a periodical allowance. This application is made on 1st September 1977 and is granted on 5th September 1977. If Mrs Z then suspects that her husband, Mr Z, is going to, or has sold, his flat in order to avoid paying the periodical allowance she can apply to the court to prevent or nullify that transfer at

any time up to 5th September 1978 (one year after settlement of the claim). If her husband had, in fact, sold the flat,
then, so long as the sale took place within the three years
prior to 1st September 1977, it could be cancelled by the
court.

It is not necessary to become overburdened with the complicated details and provisions, provided that one remembers
that the court can prevent a transfer of property if it is made
with the intention of defeating a claim for a financial
provision. If it is ever felt that moves are being made to avoid
payment of an award made under a court order it is advisable
to consult a solicitor to see what can be done to prevent this.

Sources of Help

Scottish Marriage Guidance Council
58 Palmerston Place
Edinburgh
031–225 5006
—and local branches

Scottish Catholic Marriage Advisory Centre
18 Park Circus
Glasgow
041–332 4914
—and local branches

Citizens' Advice Bureaux

Solicitors

Social Work Department of the District Councils

Help for single parents:

Gingerbread
38 Berkeley Street
Glasgow
041–248 6840

Scottish Council for Single Parents
44 Albany Street
Edinburgh EH1 3QR
031–556 3899

National Council for the Divorced and Separated
13 High Street
Little Shelford
Cambridge

For further information and reading see pages 47–8.

WILLS

Scots law recognises the right of the individual to make a Will[1] regulating the succession to his estate after his death. The age of majority is eighteen, but minors (boys over fourteen, and girls over twelve) have the same power as adults to leave a Will. Children below these ages cannot make a valid Will, nor can insane persons, although a Will made during a lucid interval may be valid, and, if the insanity takes the form of delusions, a Will may be valid if it can be shown that the delusions had no effect on its terms.

The Will must be in writing.[2] It can be printed, typed or handwritten, and can be in any language or code, including braille and shorthand. It must be signed by the person making it (the 'testator') unless he is blind or for some other reason unable to write, in which case it can be signed on behalf of the testator by a Notary Public, solicitor, Justice of the Peace, or minister acting as a notary in his own parish. A holograph Will (one written entirely in the testator's own handwriting) is valid if signed at the foot, and witnesses to the signature are not required. Most Wills are, however, prepared by solicitors, and are typewritten. In such cases, certain formalities have to be complied with when signing the document. Usually the testator signs at the foot of each page in front of two witnesses over the age of fourteen. The witnesses sign on the last page only. It is essential that the witnesses are not beneficiaries under the Will, as this might raise problems of whether or not the witnesses have influenced the testator to sign against his wishes. The testator may sign without witnesses if he writes, above his signature, the words 'adopted as holograph', which means that the Will is to have the same effect as if it had been in his own handwriting.

It is possible to buy printed forms of Wills in which one has

[1] The word 'Will' is not a technical term in Scots law. 'Testamentary Writing' is more correct, but for the purposes of this book we use the term 'Will' throughout.

[2] There is one historical exception to this rule: a verbal legacy of up to £100 Scots (£8.33 Sterling) is valid.

merely to fill in the various blank spaces with the names and addresses of beneficiaries and the amounts of legacies. Such Wills will be valid if they are attested (signed and witnessed as described above) or adopted as holograph, but it is not sufficient merely to sign them, unless, ignoring the printed parts, the handwritten portions are sufficient by themselves to form a valid holograph Will. In any event, a Will prepared by a solicitor can be more easily tailored to suit the individual's wishes than a printed form. There is no set form of words which a Will need take, provided it is quite clear from its content that it is intended to be a Will, and provided the beneficiaries and bequests are clearly identified. The printed forms of Wills often have the words indicating intention to bequeath printed rather than handwritten, so that the handwritten parts rarely form a valid holograph Will by themselves. The other danger of these forms is that they are generally printed in England and couched in terms of English, rather than Scots, law.

It is important to remember that the way in which a testamentary writing is framed may effect the Capital Transfer Tax charge on the estate. This is especially true where a husband wishes to provide for his widow, or a wife for her surviving husband, as well as their children. It is an extremely complex field and cannot be adequately covered in a book of this size, but it is a further good reason for taking professional advice when you consider making a Will.

We talk of the freedom of a person to make a Will, but, in practice, there are considerable restrictions on your liberty to direct what should happen to your estate after your death. For instance, a testator is unable to disinherit his or her spouse and children, and a Will may be invalid if it is not properly executed. It is worth noting that certain types of legacies or bequests will not be implemented by a court. Provisions which are illegal, wasteful, contrary to good morals or public policy will be struck at. An example of such an objectionable legacy would be a bequest to a wife, given on condition that she left her husband. In one case in 1927, the court struck down a clause in a Will by which the testator directed that property in Musselburgh belonging to him should be demolished, and replaced by a huge statue of himself on horseback.[1]

[1] *Aitken's Trustees* v. *Aitken* 1927 SC374.

The Scots law of succession has provided for the situation where a person makes a Will at a time when he or she has no children, but forgets to make alterations to take account of the subsequent birth of children. The children can challenge the Will, which will be cancelled on the assumption that the testator would not have wanted the Will to stand in these altered circumstances. This assumption also operates where there are children at the time of the making of the Will, but others are born later.

It is impossible to lay down guidelines on what to watch out for if you are attempting to make a Will yourself. The best way to ensure that your Will accurately reflects your wishes, is to have it drawn up by a solicitor, who is able to explain its various clauses and frame the document to suit your particular requirements. It is certainly advisable to make a Will if you buy a house, even if a building society 'owns' 90 per cent of it. Over the years the amount of your loan reduces, and, if recent trends continue, the value of the house may increase enormously, to the extent that your estate at death may be liable for Capital Transfer Tax (at present this starts at £25,000). You may be able, by a Will, to plan ahead and reduce the amount of tax payable on your death, or at least defer it until the death of your spouse, who, if no provision is made, might have to sell the house in order to pay the tax. Tax planning is, however, a subject too complex for this book and one in which it is usually well worth the expense of expert professional assistance, either from a solicitor or a chartered accountant.

Intestate Succession

A person who does not leave a valid Will is said to die 'intestate'. Most people do not make Wills, and the law has had to provide rules of succession to intestate estates. The bulk of the modern law on this topic is contained in the Succession (Scotland) Act 1964, as amended by later legislation. Until 1964, if a man died his house went automatically to his eldest son, who could, if he chose, put his mother out of the house. The fundamental changes of 1964 provide protection for the widowed spouse, and now all children, including those who are illegitimate and adopted, are treated equally.

Prior Rights

After Capital Transfer Tax and other debts have been paid, the surviving spouse is entitled to claim from the estate the dwelling-house of the deceased up to the value of £30,000, its furnishings and plenishings up to the value of £8,000, and a cash payment of £16,000 (this is reduced to £8,000 if there are children of the deceased or their descendants). The surviving spouse must have been ordinarily resident in the house at the time of the death. These rights are known as 'prior rights'. The figures for prior rights are fairly generous and in most cases prior rights will take up the entire estate without anything going to the children, as prior rights are taken off before 'legal rights' (see next section). They are designed to further the presumed wish of the deceased that the widowed spouse should be able to live on in the house with as little disturbance as possible. It should be stressed, however, that prior rights do not apply where the deceased has left a valid Will, nor in the case of a death before 10th September 1964 (the date when they were introduced). Completely different rules of intestate succession were in operation before then. To avoid complexity we will not consider these, as the estates of persons dying before 10th September 1964 will, in all probability, have been wound up by now.

For present purposes, a more important date is 23rd May 1974, when the Succession (Scotland) Act of 1973 came into force. It increased the figures for prior rights to their present levels. Before then the figure for the dwelling-house was £15,000, for furnishings it was £5,000, and the cash payment was also £5,000 (reduced to £2,500 if the deceased was survived by children or their descendants).

Legal Rights

In Scotland, it is impossible for a man or woman to leave a Will completely disinheriting his or her spouse or children. By a rule dating from earliest times, they are guaranteed certain 'legal rights' in the moveable estate of their deceased spouse or parent, that is, in any estate which is other than land and buildings, whether or not the deceased left a Will. If there is no Will, prior rights are deducted before legal rights, and there may be no estate left out of which to deduct legal rights.

If there is a Will, it is up to the surviving spouse and children to decide whether they are better off accepting any provisions in their favour in the Will rather than claiming legal rights, as they cannot do both.

The right of the widow or widower is to one-third of the moveable estate, if there are children of the deceased—natural, adopted, legitimate or illegitimate—or their legitimate descendants. If there are no surviving children or descendants, the right is to one-half of the moveables.

Together, the deceased's children are also entitled to one-third of the net moveable estate, if there is a surviving spouse, and to one-half if there is not. Illegitimate and adopted children can also claim legal rights, and the legitimate descendants of any child of the deceased are entitled to the share which their parent would have received.

Legal rights can be claimed from the moveable estate which is left after Capital Transfer Tax, other debts and, where appropriate, prior rights have been deducted.

The Remaining Estate

When prior rights and legal rights have been paid in full, the remaining estate is available for division according to the rules of intestate succession. The Succession (Scotland) Act sets out the order in which relations rank as intestate heirs. The general rule is that property descends through the family. Surviving children, whether legitimate, illegitimate or adopted, have the right to the remaining estate. If some of the children predecease their parents, then their legitimate issue are entitled to their share. If no children survive, any grandchildren are next in line.

If there are no descendants, the remaining estate is divided between the brothers and sisters and the parents of the deceased. The parents are entitled to one-half between them, the brothers and sisters sharing the other half. If there are no parents, the brothers and sisters succeed to the entire estate, and vice versa.

If no descendants, parents, or brothers and sisters survive, the deceased's spouse is entitled to the remaining estate. This may seem a long way down the list, but he or she is adequately provided for by prior rights, and is also entitled to legal rights, which are taken off before the remaining estate is divided.

Next in the rank of succession are uncles and aunts; then grandparents, then brothers and sisters of grandparents; and so on to more remote relations. In the absence of surviving relatives, any remaining estate of an intestate goes to the Crown.

Testate Succession

Prior rights only apply on intestacy, but the surviving spouse and children of the deceased are entitled to claim legal rights, whether or not their spouse or parent left a Will. Legal rights are only taken out of the moveable estate, and at most take up two-thirds of that (the surviving spouse and children each take one-third). The entire heritable estate and the remaining one-third of the moveable estate can be disposed of according to the deceased's will, and, as many estates comprise a house (heritable) and a bank account (moveable) and personal effects, two-thirds of the moveables may not represent a large proportion of the total estate.

Where a Will leaves nothing to the surviving spouse and children, they will invariably claim legal rights, but where they are provided for in the Will, they must choose whether to accept the provisions in their favour or to reject them and claim legal rights instead. Scots law does not allow them to do both. The position is usually resolved by deciding which will leave the spouse and/or children better off. Happily, problems of this nature arise rarely.

Executries

Executors

An executor (executrix if a woman) is the person appointed to administer the estate of a deceased person. A Will usually names at least one executor to carry out its purposes, and such a person is called an Executor-Nominate. In cases of intestacy the Sheriff Court appoints the executors, and in this case they are called Executors-Dative. The executor's title or authority to realise the deceased's estate and distribute the proceeds among the beneficiaries is derived from a document called Confirmation which is obtained from the Sheriff Court of the area where the deceased was domiciled. In the case of a person dying in Scotland, but not domiciled in any particular Sheriff Court district, or dying outside Scotland but leaving estate here, Confirmation is issued by the Commissary Court in Edinburgh.

Who is Entitled to be Executor?

Where the deceased has left a valid Will and appointed one or more executors, there is no problem, provided that at least one of the executors is still alive when he dies. Where there is no Will, the person primarily entitled to be Executor-Dative is the surviving spouse, as he or she is entitled to prior rights. Prior rights, as we saw earlier, often take up the entire estate, but if there is estate left after their deduction, the intestate heirs are entitled to be appointed along with the surviving spouse. If there is no surviving spouse, the intestate heirs can claim the office. They are entitled to the office in the same order in which they are entitled to inherit the intestate estate, that is children (including those adopted and illegitimate), if there are no children, the surviving parent or parents of the deceased, together with brothers and sisters or their legitimate issue (full brothers and sisters and their descendants are preferred to half-brothers and half-sisters and their issue), and so on to more remote relations.

The Procedure for Winding Up an Estate

To appoint an Executor-Dative a Petition should be presented to the Sheriff Court or Commissary Court in Edinburgh, as appropriate. This is almost invariably prepared by a solicitor and a copy can be inspected at the office of the Sheriff Court, or, where required, Commissary Clerk. If no competing claims to the office are made, the Sheriff grants the Petition and confirms the pursuer Executor-Dative. This is done by the Sheriff 'in Chambers', and nobody need appear in court to give evidence.

At this stage, an Inventory of the deceased's estate is presented to the court for Confirmation to be issued. Again, this is usually framed by the solicitor. He will go through the deceased's papers to ascertain what estate is left, and what debts the deceased had. This will involve writing to any banks or building societies where it is thought there are accounts, to find out the balances at the date of death, and to insurance companies for valuations of policies. Holdings of premium bonds, savings certificates, and so on, will also have to be confirmed. Stocks and shares will have to be valued, as will any heritable property, jewellery, motor-cars, furniture and personal effects; and any repayment of income tax will have to be estimated. All this must go in the Inventory. When it is completed, the executor takes an oath in front of a Justice of the Peace or Notary Public that it is correct.

If the estate is large enough to be liable to Capital Transfer Tax, the Inventory is sent to the Inland Revenue with a cheque for the tax payable. This step is taken before Confirmation is issued. Until its issue, the executor has no authority to deal with the estate and it will generally be necessary to obtain bank overdraft facilities to pay any Capital Transfer Tax. The Inland Revenue return the Inventory, endorsed with a receipt for the tax.

When the Inventory is ready to present for Confirmation the Executor-Dative must be able to guarantee to the court that he will pay out the estate to those entitled. This is usually done by obtaining from an insurance company a Bond of Caution to the value of the deceased's gross estate. The insurance company will charge a single premium for the policy.

When the formalities have been completed, Confirmation is issued. This is a photocopy of the Inventory with the court's certificate attached. It gives the executor the right to ingather and realise the estate, pay off any debts or overdraft, and pay out the net estate to those entitled to it. The Confirmation is sent round all the banks, companies, insurance companies, etc., who will then pay out the sums due to the estate. Sometimes they are prepared to pay without requiring Confirmation, usually only when the amount is very small. They cannot be compelled to dispense with Confirmation, as this is their assurance that they are paying out the funds to the correct person.

Circulating the Confirmation can take quite a long time if there are several items in the Inventory, and it is possible to obtain, at a small charge, Certificates of Confirmation as well as the main document. Each Certificate applies to one item of estate only, and they enable the executor or solicitor to ingather the estate much more quickly. This will be advantageous if there is a bank overdraft to be cleared.

The duties of the executor are to pay off the debts, pay out any prior rights, satisfy claims for legal rights, and distribute the remaining estate in terms of the deceased's Will, or, in intestate estates, among the intestate heirs of the deceased. His office comes to an end when he has accounted for the amount of funds in the Inventory. Further negotiation with the Capital Taxes office may be necessary, and it is common, finally, to obtain from them a certificate stating that there are no outstanding claims for Capital Transfer Tax.

The procedure for obtaining Confirmation is slightly different in the case of an Executor-Nominate. The Petition for appointment is unnecessary, so also is the Bond of Caution, but the Will must be submitted with the Inventory for Confirmation. On the death of a testator it is common to register his or her Will in the Books of Council and Session for preservation as a public record. If this is done, the original is retained by the Keeper of the Registers, but, on payment of a small fee, an Extract can be obtained, which will be accepted by the Sheriff Court or Commissary Court. Otherwise the procedure is the same as that for appointing an Executor-Dative.

In the case of small estates (those under £3,000 gross *and* under £1,000 net, i.e. when debts have been deducted), Confirmation can be obtained more simply. The Sheriff Clerk or Commissary Clerk will prepare an Inventory, take the necessary oath and issue Confirmation. In intestate estates where this procedure is adopted, there is no need for the Petition, but the Bond of Caution is still required and the executor must produce evidence of identity and of relationship to the deceased. If there is a Will, this must be produced, together with sufficient proof of identity.

Winding up an estate can be a lengthy process and may take several months to complete. The fee which a solicitor charges for the executry will generally depend on the size of the estate and the amount of work involved. In addition, there is a fee to be paid when the Petition is presented, and 'commissary dues' are also charged when the Inventory is lodged for Confirmation. These dues cover the expense of handling the relevant papers, and vary according to the amount of the estate.

Trusts

A testator often wishes to make special provisions in his Will. He may wish to give his wife the use of his estate during her lifetime, after which it is to go to his children, or he may state that legacies are only to be paid when the beneficiaries reach a certain age, or marry—the variations are limitless. To do this, the deed, usually called a Trust Disposition and Settlement, sets up a trust and appoints trustees to carry out its provisions. It may be many years before the purposes of the trust have been fulfilled and, if you are appointed a trustee, as opposed to a mere executor, you may find yourself involved in considerably more work, although the solicitor will carry out most of the administrative duties. In many cases, the solicitor will have been appointed as one of the trustees to help administer the trust, and, of course, nobody can be compelled to accept office as a trustee. However, if you accept office you must carry out the duties set out in the Trust Deed as far as possible. A trustee who neglects his duties may find that he is personally liable to the beneficiaries under the Trust Deed for any loss that ensues, and there is an absolute prohibition against a trustee purchasing any of the trust's estate, or dealing with it in any way whereby his personal interest might conflict with his duty as a trustee.

The field of trusts is extremely specialised and too wide to be adequately covered in a book of this size. Suffice it to say that the essential difference from an executry is that the estate is not simply ingathered, realised and distributed. A trust is of a continuing nature, and involves management of the trust funds, including their investment in government and other stocks and shares, the running of bank and building society accounts, transfer of investments to maintain the value of the estate in accordance with the directions in the Trust Deed; nor

Not all trusts come into operation on death, and it is still common to set up trusts during one's lifetime, for one reason or another. Much of the law on trusts is now statutory, and regulation controls the type of investment in which trustees may place trust funds. This is to preserve the fund rather than risk its being seriously diminished by speculative investment. The trustees cannot carry out acts which are outside the remit of their appointment, as their duty is to administer the trust estate in accordance with the directions in the Trust Deed; nor can a trustee make any profit out of his office. This means that a trustee acting as solicitor for the trust cannot charge for his professional services unless the Trust Deed specifically authorises it, though as most Trust Deeds are prepared by solicitors a clause entitling them to charge their usual professional remuneration is usually contained in the deed.

THE HOME

Ownership of Land and Buildings

The system of land-holding in Scotland is called the 'feudal system'. The theory of this is that all land in Scotland is held 'of the Crown', i.e. that the Crown is the ultimate owner or Superior.[1] Centuries ago, the monarch would give grants of pieces of land to his nobles and loyal servants and these 'Charters' often contained conditions binding the nobleman to particular services or feu-duties, such as providing troops for the king's army. In turn, the nobleman might make similar grants of land, and so the chain would progress. The person at the end of this chain was referred to as the 'vassal' (the person we think of as the owner), and the person to whom the services were provided was, and still is, known as the 'Superior'.

A simple modern-day structure might be as follows:

The Crown

Duke or Earl   Crown Charter

Building Contractor   Feu Charter

Proprietor   Feu Disposition
(vassal)

Purchaser   Disposition

[1] In Orkney and Shetland land may be held under 'udal tenure' which means that it has not been feudalised by the proprietors obtaining a title or Charter from the Crown. The land was held by possession without any written title.

The feudal system will ultimately be replaced by a simpler system of land-holding. The first steps have already been taken and, as a result of the Land Tenure Reform (Scotland) Act 1974, feu-duties (the annual payment by the vassal to the Superior) can be redeemed at Whitsunday (15th May) and Martinmas (11th November), these being the two dates in the year when feu-duties are normally paid. There is also now, with a few exceptions, compulsory redemption of feu-duties when a house or flat is sold. Although feu-duties are being extinguished the other conditions in the various Feu Charters and Feu Dispositions remain unaffected and, of course, are still important.

Recording of Deeds

Unlike the transfer of moveable items such as furniture, the transfer of land or buildings cannot be made in an informal manner. Prior to 1617 when an Act of the Scots Parliament introduced a Register of Deeds, earth and stones were handed over to symbolise the transfer of ownership. Since that date the Register has developed into what is now called the General Register of Sasines in H.M. Register House in Edinburgh. It is divided into one section for each county and, as each property has its own individual Search Sheet, it is possible to trace the owner of any particular area of ground or building in the country. In the event of a dispute between two people as to true ownership the Search Sheet is conclusive and the person whose title is recorded first will be the legal owner. Whenever a property is sold the seller's solicitors will instruct a search in the Register in order to satisfy the purchaser that the person selling the property is in fact the owner. If the seller already has a mortgage there will be recorded security deeds, and the search will also ensure that the seller has repaid the loan and that the appropriate deed has been recorded discharging the loan.

House Purchase

In this field there are a multitude of differing needs and requirements. Some people require the minimum of assistance with financing the purchase and others require detailed financial arrangements in order to enable them to purchase the property.

For most people the building society is the provider of funds, and we shall assume this to be the case in our treatment of buying a house.

Where to Find a House

This is not difficult. In Scotland a large proportion of house purchase and sale work is still carried on by the legal profession, so it will often be a solicitor who is advertising the property on behalf of his client. He will advertise the properties he is selling either in the local or national press, or in a Solicitors' Property Centre, or merely on his own office notice-board. The advertisements will usually be small, as space costs a considerable amount, and, as often as not, will not mention the price. This latter point often causes ill-will as it is particularly frustrating for a purchaser not to be immediately advised of the full facts concerning the property in which he is interested. In country areas it will be exceptional for the price to be shown in the press advertisement and only local pressure will be able to alter this. One reason put forward for not disclosing the price in the advertisement is that, particularly if you live within a small community, your friends and neighbours will immediately know the market-value of your property.

The other main activist within the field of house purchase is the estate agent, who can either be a professionally qualified chartered surveyor or simply an individual who chooses to set himself up in the business of buying and selling property for other people. The influence of estate agents is becoming greater in Scotland and one is increasingly aware of their presence. They will also advertise the property in both local and national press, usually under a block advertisement which bears their own name in bold print, and you will also be able to peruse files of properties within their offices.

There is no need to approach either of these bodies when you are thinking of purchasing, as it is perfectly feasible for you to come to an arrangement with a seller directly. It can safely be said that of all parts of the system of purchasing a house the least difficult is finding the houses which are available and from which you must make your choice. To find the ideal house is a different question.

Finance

Having found a suitable house the major consideration is finance. Can I afford it? It is difficult to lay down a definite rule on this as circumstances can differ so widely. For the first-time buyer it is a relatively simple question to answer as he will know exactly the amount of his savings and also the figure he is prepared to spend on the purchase. For the existing house owner it is not so easy, as what he will be able to pay will depend on how much he receives from his own house, rather like a merry-go-round. This is the time to be advised. The advice can come from several quarters: a solicitor, a bank manager, an estate agent or an insurance broker, being a few. Solicitors do not have a monopoly of the house-purchase system, but they do account for a large proportion of it. Before an individual can become the legal owner of a property he will have to have a recorded title to it, and only a solicitor may sign the necessary registration for this. Apart from practical limitations there is nothing to prevent one from doing all one's own conveyancing should one so wish, but it is generally advisable not to do so unless one has professional experience or assistance.

Regardless of where you finally obtain your advice you will have to pay fees and government duties. These should not be ignored when considering how to finance the purchase as they can form a substantial amount. The purchase itself may be financed in a number of ways but it is important to ensure at the early stage that sufficient funds will be available. We shall look into the methods of finance shortly but for the moment we shall assume that your arrangements have been made.

Surveying the Property

The next important requirement is for the house to be surveyed by a professional chartered surveyor. Whether or not one is using a building society it is advisable to do this, and the cost involved is minimal compared with the total purchase price of the property. If the building society has the largest financial stake in the house a report is made on their instruction, and you, as the prospective purchaser, have no direct recourse to the society's valuer or valuation. The contract is between the surveyor or valuer and the building society, and you have no contractual right to sue the surveyor if his survey is in error. This is an important point which is often overlooked by the public. However it is perfectly in order for you to instruct your own survey report and in many instances this is advisable.

The Offer

If all is well with the property, you are in a position to submit an offer. The offer will not be binding on both parties unless it is in writing, and it is usual for a solicitor to prepare this document, although once again there is no reason why you should not do so yourself should you so wish. You either submit the offer as soon as possible or alternatively you submit it on a 'closing date'. In either case it must be remembered that an offer is binding as soon as it has been accepted and the contract is complete. You cannot submit offers for several properties at the one time and then pull out of those which do not attract you. Unlike the system in England, the offer and acceptance form the end of the chain and all that follows thereafter is the legal spade-work and completion procedure. You are committed at the start.

One of the most difficult parts of the whole purchase transaction is assessing how much to bid for the house. When prices are rising rapidly one view is that one should offer the most one can afford as, by so doing, you will not be too disappointed if the offer turns out to be unsuccessful. This is no real consolation however. A chartered surveyor or solicitor can advise you as to the tactics, because there are most definitely advantages and disadvantages to the various methods which can be used. In some instances speed is essential for success whereas on other occasions it will make little difference. Know how much you can afford to pay, how much the property is worth and how much you want it, and with those guidelines in mind seek advice as to how best to submit your offer.

If your immediate offer is accepted, good and well; if not you may find that a 'closing date' has been fixed and your offer will be considered then, along with any other offers which may subsequently be received. Because of the interest which has been shown in the property, the seller has decided to allow all those who are interested to submit their offers.

Once these have all been received he will make his decision. While the successful offer is usually the one which offers the highest price this need not be the case. Other points can have a direct bearing on the successful outcome of your offer, such as the date on which you want to take possession.

Your offer can take whatever form it likes—it can be detailed or brief—but the essential conditions of price, property and date of entry must all be there. It is better for it to be more detailed than brief as this can avoid subsequent complications, but the form will depend upon the circumstances of each particular prospective purchase. If, for instance, the property is a tenemental flat it may well be important to insert a condition to the effect that you do not have more than your own share of the upkeep of the roof or other common parts. If the property is an isolated cottage in the country you must ensure that you will have adequate access to it, and this should be considered when the offer is drafted. All this is not to say that the offer is a complicated document but it should indicate that there are areas where difficulties can arise, and if one is to avoid these it is best to seek advice.

If your offer is accepted then you will receive a written reply which can either be unqualified or contain further conditions which you can choose to accept or reject. In normal circumstances there is little additional correspondence and the offer is usually accepted in an unqualified manner. When that has been done the contract has been completed and the house is yours.

The great attribute of this system is speed. One can submit an offer for acceptance as soon as the house is advertised on the market and the whole deal can be clinched within twenty-four hours. The system is not complicated and generally it works to the advantage of both parties. As the market changes so will the style of purchase alter and what may prove successful in a slack market may not prove so successful when the market is rising rapidly.

So far the procedure can be carried out without the services of a solicitor, but it is not usual to do so. Once the contract or 'missives' have been concluded the technical conveyancing formalities come into play. Although the house is effectively yours the title deeds must still be checked and the necessary deed prepared for recording in the General Register of Sasines. If you are obtaining a loan from the building society your solicitor will have to prepare all the loan papers, one of which, the Standard Security (the formal loan document), will have also to be recorded.

Payment of the purchase price has not yet been mentioned and obviously this is a very significant item. The date of entry, which is one of the more important conditions in the formal offer to purchase, is not only the date when you can occupy your house but also the date when the price has to be paid. Failure to pay on this date can lead to serious difficulties, the least of which may be that you will be liable to pay interest on the balance unpaid at a fairly punitive rate.

As buying a house is an important step in the life of the family, the actual payment procedure is usually more formal than just handing over a cheque. Settlement usually takes place in a solicitor's office between the respective solicitors and the cheque is only handed over in exchange for the keys. There might be variations in this actual exchange but generally, the one is exchanged for the other. Not unreasonably, both parties are often wary about the other's ability to meet his end of the bargain and the system is strengthened by there being a firm set of procedural rules.

Insurance

An important implication of the conclusion of the contract is that the risk of loss or damage by fire, etc., passes to the purchaser, and it is essential that he insures himself against this risk. The solicitor who acted for the purchaser used to insure the property immediately upon conclusion of the bargain, but now it is increasingly common for the building society to insure the property under a block policy, and the insurance becomes effective upon completion of the loan application form. If you are purchasing a flat in a tenement it is worth noting that for a comparatively low premium all the owners of the individual flats can take out a block insurance policy covering the whole tenement in addition to insuring their respective flats. In view of the cost of rebuilding tenements, such additional cover may be worthwhile.

Overdraft or Bridging Loan

It is not uncommon to find, as a house purchaser, that the date of entry, i.e. the date when you take entry to and pay for your new house, is earlier than the date when you hand over the keys of the house you are selling. You will, of course, be relying on the sale proceeds to pay, in part at least, for your new house, but you will only receive these proceeds when the purchaser takes entry. There will thus be a short period during which you will require temporary overdraft facilities from a bank by means of what is called a bridging loan. Also your building society's loan cheque may not arrive in time for your date of entry to your new house, and this is another situation in which a bridging loan is required. Before lending the money the bank will have to be satisfied that money will be available on a certain specified date to cover the loan which they have been requested to make. This will form the security for their loan. Once they have agreed to lend, the bank will give you a Mandate to sign which will instruct your solicitor to deliver the sale proceeds of your house direct to the bank to repay the bank loan. If the loan is to cover until receipt of the building society loan the Mandate will be altered to include delivery of the loan proceeds from the building society.

The rate of interest which is charged is usually about 4 per cent higher than the minimum lending rate, but as it is an allowable expense for tax purposes it is not as expensive as it might initially appear.

Title deeds

As explained, each owner of a house will have a recorded title to it—so in time large numbers of legal documents can accumulate for any given property. Most of the legal significance and value of these historical deeds has been eroded by legislation, but it is still important to ensure that all the appropriate title deeds are retained in safe-keeping. The title deeds may contain information on conditions which affect the property. Before the purchase is completed a solicitor will examine these to ensure that they are in order and that you are not adversely affected by them without this having been brought to your attention. This is useful and important as it provides you with a clear statement of the rights and liabilities which affect your property. Two examples of the conditions that may affect you are given on page 81.

Where there is a building society or other such loan the title deeds are delivered to the lender for retention, and they are only released when the loan has been repaid or under some appropriate undertaking to redeliver them. In other circumstances it is advisable for the deeds to be retained in the solicitor's strong-room or the bank's safe, but there is no rule as to their disposal and the individual can decide for himself.

The Cost

The cost of buying a house is not just the price you pay for it. Added to that are all the incidental costs which are incurred for whatever reason. There is a fee payable to the General Register of Sasines for recording the title deed or Disposition of the house, and for also recording the Standard Security or mortgage. In addition, if the price exceeds £15,000, stamp duty will be payable to the Inland Revenue at the rate of a $\frac{1}{2}$ per cent, rising to 2 per cent on property costing more than £30,000. Solicitor's fees will also be payable. While these vary, they are based upon a scale table of fees, and it should always be possible to obtain an estimate before you commit yourself to making the purchase. Banks usually charge a small fee for overdraft facilities, in addition to the actual interest which is payable, and you will also have to meet the cost of the valuation or survey report. You should be quite clear in your mind that you will have these additional costs to bear as, in total, they can amount to a substantial figure over and above the actual purchase price.

Essentially, then, buying a house is a simple affair, provided that one observes the basic principles. It is important to remember that the contract is completed at an early stage in the procedure and that the point of no return can be reached with remarkable rapidity. This means that one should arrange one's finance well in advance if one is to have as good as possible a chance of purchasing the property. While it is not necessary to seek advice, it is within one's interests to do so as errors can prove expensive to rectify. For all the outlay that is involved it is better to be a wise fool before the event than a poor one after it!

Mortgages

'Mortgage' is strictly speaking an English term, but it is universally used and we shall use it in this section of the book. Its equivalent in Scots law is the Standard Security, and no disrespect to these words is intended by the adoption of the English term.

The mortgage is the modern way of financing the purchase of a house—it is better than using cash as the value of money declines over the years, so one therefore cuts the end cost of the purchase. Building societies are often thought to be the only bodies that lend money solely for this purpose, but this is not correct. Local authorities, because of their obligation to provide housing, will often lend on low-value houses, and often they lend a 100 per cent of the purchase price. Their major drawback is that there can be a considerable delay in obtaining the loan as their commitment is so heavy and the number of applicants so great. The government also has a hand on the tap and can indirectly increase or decrease the amount of money which local authorities can lend for this purpose. Insurance companies will also lend but often confine their loans to existing policy-holders or prospective insurance customers. Mortgages obtained from them will be more expensive as the borrower will have to pay the mortgage repayment and also the insurance premium. They are, however, attractive to high-income earners who require larger-than-average loans because of the greater income-tax relief.

The building societies are undoubtedly the most common source of finance and their existence is geared to lending money for house purchase. The money which they borrow from the investing public is relent at a higher rate of interest and the difference between the interest rates is used to cover their running costs.

It is often advisable to 'shop around' in order to find the most suitable building society for your purposes. One building society may not be prepared to lend either because they do not feel the property is of an adequate standard or perhaps because they regard your income as being insufficient. Another building society may not find these difficulties and will be quite willing to lend, so it is well worth visiting several building societies to see who will give you the best terms.

Before a loan is made, the building society will require information about you and your general background—details of your age, income, employment, family, and even nationality will be required. Borrowers who are not in steady employment, such as persons working on commission, might find it more difficult to receive a mortgage, as also would those who have poor records of rent and debt repayment. All the required information is usually contained in the application form. This can either be completed by the borrower himself or with the assistance of the building society's clerk.

Building societies will usually lend up to between 2 and $2\frac{1}{2}$ times your annual income, and they will normally limit repayments to one-quarter of the borrower's monthly earnings. Overtime payments will not be considered in arriving at these figures, nor will the value of a company car. As explained, the property will be valued by the building society's valuer and the amount which is lent will be a percentage, usually 90 per cent, of the valuation figure. These percentages will vary according to the age and type of property concerned. If the maximum which they are prepared to lend to you is lower than the figure suggested by the valuer's report, you will have to find the full deposit from your own resources. For example, if you earn £3,000 per annum then the building society will lend up to a maximum of £7,500 ($2\frac{1}{2}$ times £3,000). If they value the property at £10,000 (90 per cent of which is £9,000) they will still lend only £7,500 and not £9,000. You will have to find the additional £2,500.

As with all rules there is a degree of inbuilt flexibility and it may be possible for you to obtain a larger amount by way of a loan but this will depend on the circumstances of the application.

To enable the borrower to obtain a slightly higher loan it is often possible to invest in a Mortgage Guarantee Policy which guarantees the repayment over the given period of years. A Mortgage Guarantee Policy is issued by a building society when they feel that the amount of the loan is perhaps higher than the valuation of the property or the income of the borrower does not fall within the standard requirements laid down by the building society. A single premium of approximately £30 will be charged.

It is not only the building societies who arrange their own

loans—there are numerous other firms who may do so on their behalf. Solicitors, estate agents and mortgage brokers all operate within this field and you have complete freedom of choice as to whom you decide to consult. Each body will offer you a different type of service, and, particularly with those who are not affiliated to some professional body, great care should be taken before committing either yourself or finance to the project.

What Type of Mortgage?

This will depend upon your personal needs and requirements and, more important, on how much you earn. Your total family income is not taken into account, but your wife's income may be, and this can substantially increase the amount of the loan which you are offered. There are three main classes of mortgage:

1 Repayment mortgages
2 Standing mortgages and endowment mortgages
3 Option mortgages

1 Repayment Mortgages

These comprise the majority of building society and local authority loans. The borrower agrees to repay a fixed sum over a fixed period of years (the term of the loan) and the lender adds loan and interest together and divides the total into equal monthly repayment instalments. As the loan declines over the years so does the amount of interest and so also does the amount of tax relief which may be obtained.

If the loan is not insured and the borrower is a married man and he dies before the loan is repaid, his widow is left to shoulder the burden of repayment. In many cases she may be unable to do this. One solution to this problem is for the borrower to take out a Mortgage Protection Policy which will cover the risk of his dying during the repayment term. While protecting his widow and children, it must be remembered that this too is an additional cost.

One disadvantage to this type of mortgage is that there may be a large difference between the amount which the society will lend and the actual price paid for the house. This means that the borrower will have to find the balance himself.

2 Standing Mortgages and Endowment Mortgages

Standing mortgages are mortgages where the capital remains unpaid or 'stands' until the end of the loan period. It is then repaid in one lump sum. These form the basis of insurance-linked mortgages.

Because you are not repaying part of the capital each month, interest is calculated on the full amount of the loan and over the whole loan period at the maximum rate. They are thus effectively more expensive than the more usual repayment mortgage but they do also attract considerably higher tax relief which tempers the total cost of the borrowing.

An endowment mortgage links a standing mortgage with life insurance cover. It enables the borrower to repay the capital sum of the loan at the end of the period out of the proceeds of the policy. The insurance policy is taken out for the amount of the loan and is designed to mature (i.e. become payable to you) at the end of the period of the building society loan. The borrower has to pay considerably more than on repayment mortgages because he has to meet the cost of consistently high interest payments and also pay the insurance premiums, but he can secure greater tax relief both on the higher interest payments and on a percentage of the value of his insurance premium.

A variation of this is a 'with profits endowment mortgage' which involves a slightly higher insurance premium but also the prospect of a cash bonus at the end of the term; in addition to the loan being repaid. Combinations are numerous and one can produce individually-tailored schemes to cater for each person's needs.

There is as well a 'decreasing endowment mortgage' which provides insurance cover for the balance of the mortgage at any one time and often provides an agreed capital sum at the end of the loan period. The advantage of this type is that it insures the borrower's mortgage and also yields an agreed capital sum or an income in case of death. Strictly speaking it is not a standing mortgage as some capital is repaid each month.

3 Option Mortgages

These are government-designed mortgages to assist those who pay little or no tax and who, therefore, cannot fully benefit from the tax relief on mortgage interest and insurance premiums. Instead of paying normal interest rates on the loan and claiming tax relief, the borrower foregoes the relief and 'opts' for a government subsidy which secures him a lower interest rate. It is roughly equivalent to a 2½ per cent cut in the interest rate.

Recently the interest rate has been altered several times and this can often lead to difficulties for a borrower. Most lenders will agree to increase the terms of repayment, provided you are young enough, as an alternative to increasing the monthly repayment figure. Similarly, most lenders will agree to add the cost of any mortgage guarantee or mortgage protection to the capital for payment, though this does have the disadvantage of the borrower having to pay increased interest.

The building society manager or some other adviser will advise you on the relative merits of each of the three types of mortgage, and it is important that you take the best advice available before committing yourself as the step is a large one. As a proviso, it should be remembered that outwith the general sphere of advisers, such as the bank manager, the building society manager or the solicitor, there are also individuals and firms of business persons and, particularly in the field of insurance, great care should be taken to choose your advisers correctly. While the impression might be otherwise, not all individuals have solely your best interests at heart! Some of the abuses which formerly existed have been greatly reduced, in particular the practice of 'commission chasing'. Borrowers should now have complete freedom of choice in opting for an endowment mortgage, and should not be directed to a particular insurance company to obtain the appropriate life policy. Similarly they should not be offered a larger advance if they use an endowment scheme rather than a straightforward repayment one.

How Long Will it Take?

This will vary with circumstances but generally speaking you should allow from six to eight weeks for the conveyancing to be completed satisfactorily. This period will commence as soon as your offer has been accepted, so the date of entry mentioned in that offer should take this into account. Transactions can be completed more quickly, but unless you are in a hurry it is advisable to let matters proceed at a more leisurely pace.

Loan arrangements take time due to the building society system; to try to cut this short will probably only result in your bearing additional expense by way of interest payments on an overdraft.

Further Advances

An indirect benefit of inflation is that as the value of money decreases so the value of your house increases. This means that there will be sufficient residual security to enable the building society or other lender to have adequate cover for any further sum which they might advance. This residual cover upon which a further advance might be made is often referred to as the 'reversion'. If additional funds are required to cover the cost of, for example, installing central heating, it is a simple matter to request the payment from the building society and the appropriate adjustment will be made to your monthly repayments. This is probably one of the best ways of acquiring additional funds, but it is also possible to obtain a second loan from other organisations, such as a bank or an insurance company. The interest rate may well be higher and care should be taken to ensure that you do not overburden yourself with too onerous a commitment.

Further Information

The Layman's Guide to Scots Law. Volume 1: 'House Purchase and Sale', Richard M. Keith and George B. Clark—Gordon Bennett Publications (2nd edition 1977) 65p.

Sources of Help

Solicitors

Solicitors' Property Centres

Local Authority Housing Departments and Housing Advice Centres

House Sale

The system for selling a house is the reverse to that of purchasing. There are, however, more options open to an individual as the choice of professional adviser is wider. The preliminary work is significantly easier and many people feel that they can do it themselves. Alternatively, the services of a solicitor, an estate agent, or a combination of both can be utilised. Advantages and disadvantages vary with each method and also, of course, with the market at the time of sale. Before considering how to proceed it is advisable to obtain impartial advice as this can save unnecessary expense at a later date—ask your local Citizens' Advice Bureau for advice; or your bank manager. For example, it may be superfluous to employ the services of an estate agent to sell a property which is in a sought-after area as the house would sell equally simply without such services.

Advertising

Advertising itself is a broad subject. A house can be sold in any number of ways, and like any other commodity it can be marketed through the services of numerous people. Market factors will play an important part in deciding the best manner of advertising and it is always advisable to examine the market closely before finally deciding the method which most suits your needs. One of the most common methods in Scotland is advertising in the national press. The national newspapers set aside pages which carry classified advertisements for different regions of the country on different days. Purchasers buy the newspaper on the appropriate day and then scan its pages to see if a suitable property can be found. It is a simple matter to instruct the advertisement and the cost will vary according to the size, measured in column inches. An average cost might be £20 per insertion but this will vary according to the newspaper and the style of advertisement. Local press is the cheapest form of press advertising and if you are looking for a very cheap method there is little to beat simply displaying a 'for sale' sign from your window or in your garden. Cost is a significant factor in advertising and it is important to word the advertisement clearly and concisely so that no unnecessary detail is included. One can seek advice on this or read other advertisements which appear in papers and gauge the appropriate style yourself.

Both estate agents and solicitors will place an advertisement for you and they will also advise on the format of the advertisement. Charges will vary—an estate agent will usually charge a 2 per cent commission on the sale price of the property for his services, in addition to charging for each insertion in the paper, whereas the solicitor might not charge a percentage but will include a block figure for advertising in his total fee. If you choose either of these advisers you should be able to obtain an estimate from them before instructing them and you will be able to work out the total cost with a fair degree of accuracy. There is nothing to prevent you advertising the house in your own name and asking for offers to be submitted to yourself as an individual. You can then go to the solicitor with an offer to purchase your house and he can proceed from there. It all depends on how committed you wish to be to the sale of your own property.

Apart from estate agents advertising properties in their offices, a recent development has been the growth of Solicitors' Property Centres. These usually exist in the High Street of large towns or cities and they are supported by local solicitors who pay a given subscription or charge each year. The centres provide the public with a collection of particulars of houses which are available for sale in that locality. The advantage of these centres to the seller is that the cost of placing details of a house on the file is small and there is a high likelihood that a sale will result as the centres attract wide attention. This again, however, is a service which can be assessed on its merits and is something which can be considered when looking at the whole overall advertising strategy.

As well as considering the manner of advertising it is important to consider how you wish the sale to be handled. For example, if the house is unoccupied it may be impossible for you to show it yourself and you will wish to employ the services of some agency to handle that side of it for you. The most common situation is where the owner is also the occupier and he himself will wish to show people around as, quite rightly, he will take the view that the owner knows most about the property and can often sell it best himself. This second point is arguable as estate agents will consider that they are experts in selling houses and so will firms of lawyers. What is required, however, is a conscientious effort at selling the property. Some houses do sell themselves but the vast majority require assistance, and nothing puts off potential purchasers more than a totally disinterested approach.

The advertisement will also usually specify times at which the house may be viewed and, for the sake of the person who is selling, this is advisable as it does concentrate the visitors to a certain time of the day. It is also useful to indicate the price which you are looking for as this will deter unnecessary callers and it also indicates the market into which you are placing the property.

The length of time over which you will advertise will depend upon the market situation at the time of your sale. Some houses will be sold following one advertisement whereas others will require some weeks before a buyer is found. This is perhaps an area where advice is useful. It is pointless to advertise a house for a short period and then give up, assuming that there is no one interested. People may be interested, but just taking time to consider your particular property.

The Offer

When you feel the house has generated sufficient interest in the market place you can fix a closing date, either yourself or through your solicitor or estate agent. The closing date should be intimated to all those parties who have expressed interest in purchasing the house, and if they are still interested they will submit an offer on that specified time and date. The closing date can be used to speed up people's interest in purchasing, but there is also the danger of losing the interested party. They might take the view that because so much interest has been expressed in the house there is little point in them attempting to submit an offer. The closing date is just one weapon which is available in the armoury of selling, but it should always be used with caution and discretion.

You may not need a closing date if you receive an offer completely out of the blue. If this offer is acceptable to you, then there is no reason at all why you need not accept it immediately. The final decision always rests with the owner as to whether or not an offer should be accepted. Both the solicitor and estate agent must take your instructions before replying to an offer, and it is quite open to you to reject one offer in favour of another without specifying your reason.

As soon as an offer has been accepted a contract is concluded and you cannot get out of it without incurring liability to pay damages—it is not open to you to consider a further offer and then reject the first one. The great advantage of the system is that there is certainty from a very early stage and there is no question of gazumping. Gazumping occurs where the seller accepts your offer, and later tells you that he has received a higher offer which you must match to prevent the seller from backing out. Happily the Scottish system goes a long way to prevent this from happening.

The offer can be accepted by you yourself but generally it is advisable to employ the services of a solicitor to do this as the conditions contained in the acceptance require careful consideration.

As soon as the owner decides to sell his property the building society should be advised so that the title deeds can be sent to the solicitor before the sale is concluded. These are required to convey the house to the purchaser and to discharge the owner's loan. It is important to remember to advise the building society at as early a stage as possible so that these formalities can be attended to without delaying the sale transaction.

It is important to know that the purchaser will meet his liability and pay the price, particularly if you then proceed to purchase another house on the strength of the money you will receive from your own sale. One can never guarantee that a purchaser will pay. In most cases he does, and it is very rare in the field of private house purchase for a purchaser not to pay the money on the appropriate day. A solicitor will investigate the identity and credit of a purchaser if requested to do so, but the information which he receives may not be all that helpful. Should the purchaser not pay the price on the given date there is very little that the seller can do as 'time is not of the essence', which means that time is not an essential condition of the contract, therefore no immediate court remedy may be taken. The only remedy available is for the seller to demand the money within a specified period, and, if it is not then paid, to proceed further with court action or alternatively resell the property. Happily this occurrence is not common.

The time between the conclusion of the bargain and the receipt of the price is spent by the solicitor in the conveyancing formalities (see p. 81), and there should be constant liaison between the solicitor and his client throughout the whole process. The seller and purchaser should come to a mutual arrangement on the sale of any items which the purchaser may wish to acquire, such as carpets and kitchen units. Payment for these items can either be handled along with the payment of the house, or separately between the respective parties.

Disputes can often arise as to who takes over the fixtures and fittings in the house or flat. If there are specific items which you wish to retain, it is vitally important that these be either excluded from the purchaser's offer or else specifically mentioned in your qualified acceptance of that offer. In the absence of any clear statement to the contrary fixtures and fittings will be taken over by the purchaser, but it is perfectly in order for the seller specifically to exclude them. It is better to do so at the beginning than to get involved in a dispute at a later date.

No government stamp duty is payable on the proceeds of the sale of a house, but a substantial sum may go on a commission on the sale proceeds. This will be looked at next.

Final Account

When the date for payment arrives, the purchaser's solicitor usually sends a cheque to the seller's solicitor, who will then repay his client's building society loan and send the balance direct to the client or to his bank, deducting his fees and outgoings. One reason for the cheque being sent to the solicitor is to prevent delays in clearing cheques from individuals whose financial background might be less stable than that of a firm of solicitors. It also lends credibility to the system, and this is an important factor.

The situation is the same if an estate agent handles the sale. He is only concerned with finding a purchaser for the property, and once this is done he hands over the transaction to the solicitor who concludes the legal formalities and, normally, completes the sale arrangements. In this situation one of the outgoings which will be deducted is the estate agent's commission on the sale. This will usually be in the region of 2 per cent of the sale price. The solicitor's conveyancing fees are fixed according to a scale of fees (see p. 23), and these can always be checked if a purchaser feels that he has been overcharged. If the solicitor has also handled the sale of the house he may charge additionally a commission on the sale. This will vary from firm to firm, but it is a maximum of $1\frac{1}{2}$ per cent of the sale price. It is not our intention to differentiate between the services of the respective professions, but those wishing to sell their house should go into the relative merits of both bodies before committing themselves to either or both of the services which are available.

Feu-duty

One item which you will see in the final account is 'Redemption of feu-duty' when you sell a property, if you have not already redeemed this voluntarily. Feu-duty may be redeemed at the time when it is normally payable (Whitsun or Martinmas) or else you may continue with your annual payment and wait until you sell the house before redeeming it. Advice about this is available from the local authority and Citizens' Advice Bureau or any solicitor.

Landlord and Tenant

The Requirements of a Lease

The lease must state the parties, the property, the rent, and duration of the let. Verbal leases of up to a year are competent, but all leases for more than one year must take the form of a 'probative writ', that is, they must be signed by the parties before witnesses. Leases of a year or more are also subject to stamp duty, which varies in amount according to the length of the lease and the rent to be charged.

Regulated Tenancies

The vast majority of tenants of furnished or unfurnished dwellings are now protected under the Rent Acts. Such tenancies are said to be 'regulated'. A list of the main exceptions is given below.

Exceptions

1 Tenancies of houses owned by local authorities or registered housing associations.
2 Tenancies where a substantial proportion of the rent is for board or attendance by the landlord.
3 Unfurnished tenancies which began before 14th August 1974.
4 Tenancies where the landlord also lives in the building provided the building is not a purpose-built block of flats such as a tenement, with the tenant in one of the flats and the landlord in another.
5 Tenancies granted to a student by a university or other college.
6 Holiday lets.
7 Dwellings where the rateable value on 23rd March 1965, or on the date when the property first appeared in the Valuation Roll, if that was after 23rd March 1965, exceeded £200.
8 Tenancies where the annual rent is less than two-thirds of the rateable value.
9 Controlled tenancies. These are tenancies dating from before 6th July 1957 where the rateable value on 27th August 1972 was under £25. We shall return to these later (see p. 100).

Security of Tenure

It is clear that in most private lettings the tenants are protected. The most important aspect of this protection is security of tenure. A protected tenant cannot be forced to leave his home, even if the lease runs out, without a court order for possession.

The Sheriff Court will automatically grant the order in the following situations:

(a) Where the landlord served written notice at the beginning of the tenancy that he was an owner/occupier and that he might, at a future date, require possession of the dwelling for his own occupation, or for occupation by a member of his family, or for his retirement. The court is *entitled* to make the order for possession even if the notice was not served, but it is only *obliged* to make the order if the appropriate notice was served.

(b) Where the house has been let for less than eight months, and where sometime within the twelve months prior to the let it has been used or let as holiday accommodation. Again the landlord must have given notice at the beginning of the tenancy that he might require possession on this ground. This exception is designed to allow you to let a house out of season and still be able to get it back for holiday letting.

(c) Where the house has been let for less than twelve months, and, at some time within the twelve months prior to the let, it has been let by a specified educational institution. This is to allow universities to let out their accommodation to non-students during vacation.

In various cases the court has discretion on whether or not to order possession. The most important of these are where the rent is in arrears, or the tenant is in breach of some other condition of the tenancy—where there has been annoyance to neighbours, immoral or illegal use of the premises, neglect by the tenant leading to deterioration of the premises or furniture, or unauthorised sub-letting of the premises. The court will also usually make the order for possession if it is a tied house where the employment has been terminated and the landlord requires the dwelling for another employee.

It is a criminal offence for a landlord to turn the tenant out without a court order. This order, with the exception of the mandatory cases (a) to (c) above, will not be made unless the court considers it reasonable and is satisfied either that suitable alternative accommodation is available, or that the landlord has established one of the discretionary grounds listed in the previous paragraph.

Before seeking a court order, the landlord must serve on the tenant a notice to quit. At least four weeks' notice must be given, and the notice must advise the tenant of his basic rights: that even after expiry of the notice, he cannot be removed without a court order; that, if it is a protected tenancy, the court will only grant the order on the grounds set out in the Rent Acts; that, if it is not a protected tenancy, the tenant may ask the Rent Tribunal to postpone the effect of the notice for six months, provided he does so before the notice expires; and that if the tenant is unsure of his rights, he can obtain advice from a solicitor, the cost of which may be paid under the Legal Aid Scheme, or from a Rent Officer, Rent Tribunal Office, Citizens' Advice Bureau or Housing Aid Centre. The notice to quit is invalid unless it contains all this information.

Not only is security of tenure afforded when the lease runs out, but, if a tenant dies, the widow or widower or other member of the family residing with the tenant at the time of, and for six months before, the tenant's death, is entitled to stay on as a statutory successor. On the death of this first successor, the tenancy passes in turn to his or her successor, but, at this point, it becomes a regulated tenancy. Thereafter the landlord is entitled to serve a notice to quit in the usual way.

Fair Rents

A further important feature of regulated tenancies is that either the landlord or the tenant can apply to a Rent Officer for a fair rent to be fixed. Rent Officers are appointed by the Secretary of State for Scotland, and they record the fair rent in the Rent Register. In assessing a fair rent, the Rent Officer will consider the state of repair, character and locality of the building, the condition of any furniture provided by the landlord, and other relevant factors, including any services provided by the landlord; but the officer cannot take into account either the fact that there may be a housing shortage in the area (which would tend to push rents up) or the personal circumstances of either party, such as the earnings of the tenant. The Rent Register can be inspected by the public, free of charge, at the Rent Office, and this may give a rough guide in advance of what figure to expect. The fair rent does not, however, include any payment of rates made by the tenant, and the landlord can charge an additional amount for this.

If either the landlord or tenant is dissatisfied with the Rent Officer's decision, there is an appeal to the Rent Assessment Committee. The Committee will themselves inspect the house, and the assessment is made all over again. There is no further appeal on the amount of rent fixed by the Committee, and this is the maximum the landlord can charge.

Once a rent is registered, it is not normally possible to have a new rent registered for a period of three years unless there has been a relevant change of circumstances, such as a substantial alteration in the state of repair, or unless both parties request the review.

If the fair rent is more than 40p per week above the rent previously paid, the increase must be phased by three annual instalments of one-third of the increase, or of 40p a week, whichever is greater, up to a maximum of £1.50 per week or £78 per year. For example, if the fair rent is £6.30 per week and the previous rent was £4.20, the increase of £2.10 must be phased over three years. The increase in the first year is to £4.90, in the second year to £5.60, and in the third year to the full £6.30. If, however, a new tenant takes on the dwelling, the increased rent can be charged in full.

It should be noted that it is not compulsory to register a rent. Indeed, in most cases, the landlord and tenant simply negotiate the rent between them. If the rent is not registered the landlord can increase it by agreement, or in terms of any provisions of the lease permitting him to do so, but the tenant still has the right to go to a Rent Officer, if he so wishes, to have a fair rent fixed.

Controlled Tenancies

The rent of a controlled tenancy (see p. 97) can only be increased by an annual amount of $12\frac{1}{2}$ per cent of any amount which the landlord has spent on improvements or repairs, or by an amount equivalent to the increase in rates, if these are paid by the landlord on behalf of the tenant.

A Resident Landlord

Tenancies where there is a resident landlord are not regulated, but there is still some measure of protection for the tenants. If the rateable value does not exceed £200, they can apply to a Rent Tribunal to determine a reasonable rent, and it is an offence for a landlord to charge more than this. The reasonable rent is effective for three years unless there is a joint application or a change of circumstances meriting review by the tribunal.

Rent Tribunal procedure is also available to the other categories of lettings excepted from the provisions of the Rent Acts allowing for the fixing of a fair rent by a Rent Officer. These categories include furnished lets by universities or colleges to students. In most cases also, the tenant can apply to the Rent Tribunal to postpone the operation of any notice to quit for up to six months, provided he makes the application before the notice expires.

Rent Book

If you are a tenant, and pay your rent weekly, your landlord must provide you with a rent book. This should contain the name and address of the landlord and should state the amount of rent, information about your security of tenure, and the fact that you may be entitled to a rent allowance from the local authority. If the rent is payable to someone other than the landlord, for example, his solicitor, this person's name and address should also be clearly stated.

Repairs

The Landlord is obliged to keep the premises wind and watertight. This means that he is liable for repairs to the roof, gutters, rhone pipes, drain pipes, external walls, and so on. The tenant is obliged to keep the interior of the premises in a good state of repair and to make good any damage or breakages during the tenancy—fair wear and tear, however, are usually excepted.

Due to restrictions of space, we have been able to cover only the main points on this subject. For further information we refer the reader to an excellent series of pamphlets issued by the Scottish Information Office and available, free of charge, from the Government Bookshop.

Local Rent Officers are also extremely good sources of useful advice, but, if you are a tenant and a problem arises, you should consult a solicitor at once—the consequences of being put out of your home are so serious, especially in a time of housing shortage. Your solicitor will advise you on your rights, and can help put matters straight if you are being unjustifiably harassed by your landlord. If you are a landlord, a solicitor is also invaluable for sorting out your rights, and we recommend that you consult a solicitor before granting a lease to ensure that it complies with the requirements we outlined at the beginning of this section, and also to arrange that the notices you are required to give before the tenancy commences are served in good time.

Further Information

Addresses of Rent Officers:
For Strathclyde, Central, Dumfries and Galloway Regions, and the Western Isles:
St Andrew's House
141 West Nile Street
Glasgow G1 2RN (041–332 6981/9)

For Lothian and Borders Region:
6–7 Coates Place
Edinburgh EH3 7AA (031–225 1200)

For Tayside and Fife Regions:
28 East Dock Street
Dundee DD1 3EY (0382–24082)

For Grampian and Highland Regions, Orkney and Shetland:
47 Holburn Street
Aberdeen AB1 6BR (0224–25288)

Further Reading

Protection Under the Rent Acts

Regulated Tenancies in Scotland—Your Rents, Rights and Responsibilities

Letting Your Own Home

Landlords and the Law

Notice to Quit

Rooms to Let

—all H.M.S.O. leaflets available free of charge. Copies can be obtained from Citizens' Advice Bureaux.

Sources of Help

Solicitors

Local Citizens' Advice Bureaux

Local Rent Officers

Shelter
6 Castle Street
Edinburgh
031–226 6347

Occupier's Liability

The law imposes certain obligations upon the occupier of premises, of which many people are probably not fully aware. The occupier owes a duty to the visitor that he will take reasonable care that the visitor will not be injured while on his property. This does not mean that he must ensure that there is no lunatic with a knife concealed behind the kitchen door, but rather it means that he will have taken sufficient care of the condition of his premises so that the visitor is not liable to suffer some injury as a result of the poor state of repair of the building. For example, you would be liable in damages if your front door fell on your visitor's head because it was improperly supported or if the window cleaner fell off your window ledge because it was faulty and had given way beneath his weight. It does not matter that you are not the owner, you still owe this obligation to anyone who enters your premises. Premises are broadly defined and include not only land and buildings but also vehicles and aircraft.

Because this is a legal obligation it is one which normally can be covered by an insurance policy. The premium for this will not amount to very much, and it is well worth the small cost incurred as it could save you from being sued for a large sum of money. As a matter of interest, you are also liable for any damage done by the family pet. Usually it is necessary to show that there has been negligence, but that does not apply in all circumstances.

Another point to be considered under this heading is nuisance. Nuisance consists in using your house in such a way that you cause continuing or repeated disturbance, interference or inconvenience to the reasonable use of adjacent property by the complainer. This, for example, could apply to the volume at which your young son plays the record player. If this causes nuisance to the neighbours they may well have a ground of complaint.

You can see that either owning a property or being directly responsible for one can be an onerous task. It is not a simple matter of merely living there; various rights and obligations stem from your occupation of these premises, and they are ones of which you should be aware. Normally incidents do not occur, but when they do they can cause considerable difficulty and expense, and it is advisable to ensure that your insurance policy covers not only your building and contents but also your liability towards third parties. You should ensure that you pay your insurance premiums properly and regularly as, if the insurance cover lapses and an accident occurs, you could be liable for a large sum.

Common Repairs

For those who live in flats it is often difficult to ensure that the standard of the property is maintained adequately by all those who live off the common stair. If, for example, the common stair is in need of repair and co-proprietors are unwilling to attend to this, you may telephone the Building Control Department of the local authority and ask them to issue a Notice on the block, requesting the proprietors to have the work carried out. If after a given time this is not done, the local authority will instruct a contractor on their behalf and the proprietors in the block will be billed for their share. This bill will bear a surcharge of approximately 5 per cent so it is not in your interest to let the situation drag on to the stage when the local authority becomes involved.

THE JOB

Legislation now protects employees from unfair dismissal, provides for payments on redundancy, regulates conditions of employment and health and safety at work, and gives protection to trade unions legitimately pursuing their activities. The modern law is mainly to be found in the following Acts of Parliament:

Redundancy Payments Act 1965
Equal Pay Act 1970
Contracts of Employment Act 1972
Health and Safety at Work Act 1974
Trade Union and Labour Relations Acts 1974–6
Sex Discrimination Act 1975
Employment Protection Act 1975
Race Relations Act 1976

We will concentrate on the problems of contracts of employment, unfair dismissal, redundancy and equal opportunities.

Contracts of Employment

The Written Statement

An employer is not bound to provide a written contract. The one exception to this is the contract of apprenticeship. Employers do, however, have to give any employees normally employed for sixteen hours or more per week written particulars of the main terms of their employment.

Exceptions

Various categories of employees need not be given written statements. The most important of these are registered dock workers engaged on dock work, Crown servants, and employees who are the husband or wife of their employer. Employees who normally work abroad need not be given the written statement during any period when they are working mainly outside Great Britain, although off-shore employees within British territorial waters and employees engaged in exploration of the seabed or sub-soil or natural resources in any British-designated area of the Continental Shelf must receive written statements.

The statement must cover the following points:

(a) The names of employer and employee.

(b) The date on which the employment began.

(c) Pay—the wage or salary, or the hourly rate, or the method of calculating pay such as piece rates. It must also state how often the employee will be paid: weekly, monthly, and so on.

(d) Any terms or conditions relating to the number of working hours.

(e) Any terms of employment relating to holiday entitlement and incapacity for work due to sickness or injury. Details of sick pay, pensions and pension schemes, if any, should be given.

(f) How much notice both parties must give, or, if the contract is for a fixed term, the date on which the contract expires.

(g) The title of the job.

The employer must also give an additional note specifying, or referring to, any disciplinary rules (apart from those relating to health and safety at work), and setting out the procedures for dealing with grievances. From 6th April 1978 the employee must be notified whether a 'contracting-out certificate', under the Social Security Pensions Act 1975, is in force. After April 1978 employers and employees must contribute to a state pension scheme, unless private pension schemes are in force which are more favourable to the employees. All major insurance companies are offering such schemes, and where these are adopted the notice of 'contracting-out' must be given.

The written statement need not set out all the information. It can refer to other documents, such as collective agreements, works' rules and notices, provided these documents are made reasonably accessible to the employees.

The statement and additional note must be given to the employee not later than thirteen weeks after the employment has begun, and it must be kept up to date. It need not be given if the employee leaves within the thirteen-week period, and it is not required in the case of persons normally employed for less than sixteen hours per week.

Employees may be asked to sign for the written statement. If this happens to you, you should ensure that you are only *acknowledging receipt* of the statement, and that you are not being asked to sign a contract of employment. A contract will usually contain all the terms of employment, whereas the written statement need contain only the main terms and conditions. If you sign anything saying that you *accept* these written terms, you may be unable to enforce any other conditions of which you were told orally. This will not be the case if you merely acknowledge receipt of a written statement.

Notice

The Contracts of Employment Act 1972 provides minimum periods of notice, according to service, which must be given, regardless of what the individual's contract may say, though if your contract of employment contains more favourable terms, these will, of course, apply. The minimum periods which the employer must give are:

1 One week, if you have been employed continuously by the employer for four weeks or more.
2 Two weeks, if you have been employed continuously by the employer for two years or more.
3 One additional week for each further complete year of continuous employment by the employer, up to twelve weeks' notice after employment for twelve years or more.

An employee must give at least one week's notice if he has been employed for four weeks. This period does not increase with longer service, although it may be lengthened by the terms set out in the contract of employment.

Exceptions

These requirements for minimum notice do not apply where the period of employment is to be less than twelve weeks, nor to the various categories of workers excepted from the written particulars requirement noted above (see p. 105), nor to persons employed on a fixed-term contract, unless the fixed term is for four weeks or less but is then renewed so that the employee remains for twelve weeks or more.

Unfair Dismissal

An employee has a right not to be dismissed unfairly. Dismissal is either, (a) the termination, with or without notice, of the employee's contract of employment by the employer; or (b) termination by the employee himself in circumstances in which the employer's conduct entitles him to terminate the contract with or without notice; or (c) where a contract for a fixed term expires without being renewed, except where the fixed term is two years or more and the employee has agreed in writing to forego his right to complain of unfair dismissal on the expiry of the contract.

If the employer makes changes in the conditions of employment, rendering them less favourable to the employee, an Industrial Tribunal may hold that the employer has repudiated the contract—which is therefore terminated—and dismissed the employee.

An employee complaining to an Industrial Tribunal must prove that he has been dismissed, but, having done this, the onus is then on the employer to show that the dismissal was fair. In other words, the employee need not actually prove that his dismissal was unfair. The dismissal will usually be fair if the principal reason for it is related to the employee's conduct, capability or qualifications. 'Capability' is determined by reference to skill, aptitude, health or other physical or mental quality necessary to do the job. Dismissal will also be fair if it is due to redundancy (unless the employee can show that he was unfairly selected for redundancy), or if there is some other substantial reason to justify dismissal, though it would fall to the employer to establish such a reason.

Even if the employer shows that the reason for dismissal was fair, he must still satisfy the tribunal that it was reasonable in all the circumstances to dismiss the employee. If dismissal was, for example, due to misconduct, it would be unreasonable not to give the employee an opportunity to explain his conduct, and it might be unfair not to have given him a previous warning.

Exceptions

Certain categories of workers are not covered by the unfair dismissal provisions. The most important of these are persons who have not completed twenty-six weeks' continuous employment, men over sixty-five or women over sixty, and part-time employees working less than sixteen hours per week. However, if the dismissal was for an inadmissible reason (see p. 110), the above exceptions do not apply.

An employee who is the husband or wife of the employer is not covered by the unfair dismissal provisions. Members of the police and armed forces and dock workers engaged on dock work are among the other excluded categories. There are also special provisions in relation to employees working outside Great Britain. In general they are not covered, although most merchant seamen serving on ships at British ports are protected, as are most employees on off-shore installations within British territorial waters and employees engaged on work connected with exploration or exploitation of mineral resources in British-designated areas of the Continental Shelf.

Pregnancy

It is automatically unfair to dismiss a woman because she is pregnant, unless her condition makes it impossible for her to continue to do her job adequately, or unless either she or her employer would be breaking the law if she worked while pregnant. Radiologists are an example of the latter. The employer must still offer her suitable alternative employment if it is available. The employee has the right to return to her job at any time up to twenty-nine weeks after the baby's birth, provided she worked up to the eleventh week before the baby was due, and provided that, by that time, she had been working for the employer for at least two years.

Industrial Disputes

It is not regarded as unfair to dismiss an employee during a strike or lock-out or other industrial action, unless the employee can show that at least one fellow employee who took part in the dispute either was not dismissed or was offered re-engagement. This exception is designed to prevent unfair selection for dismissal, such as dismissal of ring-leaders only.

Membership of Trade Unions

An Inadmissible Reason

Dismissal is automatically unfair if the main reason for it was that the employee was a member of, or proposed to join, an independent trade union, that is, a union not controlled by his employer; or that he had taken part, or proposed to take part, at any appropriate time, in its activities; or that he refused to join a non-independent trade union. 'At any appropriate time' means at any time when the employee is not actually required to be working, e.g. during the lunch break or, if there is an agreement with the employer covering his participation in union activities, any time set out in that agreement. Such dismissals are said to be for an 'inadmissible reason'.

If there is a 'closed shop' agreement with a trade union, it is normally automatically *fair* to dismiss an employee for refusing to join, or threatening to leave that trade union. There is one main exception to this: the employee's dismissal is automatically unfair if he or she genuinely objects on grounds of religious belief to belonging to any trade union whatsoever.

Racial Discrimination

It is unlawful to dismiss someone on the grounds of colour, race, ethnic or national origins. Separate proceedings can follow under the Race Relations Act 1976, but the unfair dismissal procedure can also be invoked by the employee.

Sex Discrimination

It is unlawful to dismiss someone because of his or her sex, or because he or she is married. Once again, the employee can complain of unfair dismissal.

Making a Complaint

If you wish to complain of unfair dismissal, you should do so without delay. Any complaint must be made within three months following the date on which the termination takes effect. In the case of a fixed-term contract, the effective date of termination is the date on which it expires without being renewed. The complaint goes to the local Industrial Tribunal and the employee applies to the tribunal for reinstatement, re-engagement, or compensation. A copy of the application is sent to a Conciliation Officer of the Advisory, Conciliation and Arbitration Service (A.C.A.S.), who will try to promote a settlement if both parties request it.

Remedies

The Industrial Tribunal will decide whether reinstatement or re-engagement is practical and appropriate. Reinstatement involves a return to the original job, whereas re-engagement is a return to work for the same employer, but normally in a different job. If the tribunal considers the employee partly to blame, re-engagement is more likely to be ordered if practical. The alternative remedy is compensation – a basic award of up to £2,400, depending on age and length of service, and a compensatory award of up to £5,200 for the loss suffered by the employee, to the extent that the employer is responsible for that loss. There is an additional award of compensation if the employer has failed to comply with a tribunal's order for reinstatement or re-engagement, unless the employer can show that it was not possible for him to comply with the order. This award is thirteen to twenty-six weeks' pay, up to £2,080. If the dismissal was for an inadmissible reason (see p. 110), or was unlawful under the Race Relations Act 1976 or Sex Discrimination Act 1975, the additional award is twenty-six weeks' pay to fifty-two weeks' pay, up to a maximum of £4,160. Most awards of compensation will fall considerably short of these maximum figures.

The field of unfair dismissal is extremely complex. We have been able to cover the main points only, and we recommend for further information the booklet entitled *Dismissal— Employees' Rights*, published by the Department of Employment.

Redundancy

An employee dismissed because of redundancy is entitled to a payment from his employer, who can recover 50 per cent of the payment from the Redundancy Fund, which is financed by an allocation from the social security contributions the employer pays in respect of employed earners.

Exceptions

Most classes of employees are covered by these provisions. The main exceptions are:

1 A person who is the husband or wife of the employer.
2 Crown servants.
3 Registered dock workers engaged on dock work.
4 Employees who normally work outside Great Britain or Northern Ireland, unless they are there in accordance with the employer's instructions, and the contract is terminated.

Self-employed persons are, of course, not eligible.

Redundancy arises in the following situations:

1 Where the employer has ceased, or intends to cease, to carry on the business; or has ceased, or intends to cease to carry on the business at the place at which the employee was contracted to work;

or

2 where the employer's requirements for employees of a particular kind have ceased or diminished, or are expected to do so; or the requirements for such employees at the place at which they were contracted to work have ceased or diminished, or are expected to do so.

The dismissal must be wholly or mainly due to redundancy otherwise the employee is not entitled to the payment. If the employee is offered alternative work on the same terms, or if he refuses such an offer, he has no right to a payment, unless he has reasonable grounds for refusal. If the alternative work is on different terms, the employee can try it for four weeks (a longer period may be agreed if retraining is necessary) to decide whether it is suitable. If he gives notice during this period he is treated as if he had been dismissed when the old job ended, and entitlement to a payment will depend on whether refusing the offer was unreasonable. The suitability of the alternative work, the employee's skills, the rate of pay compared to previous earnings, will all be taken into account when assessing this.

If an employee is laid off or put on short-time, he may be entitled to a redundancy payment. He must have been laid off or kept on short-time either for four consecutive weeks, or for a broken series of at least six weeks within a thirteen-week period, and he must give his employer notice of his claim, within four weeks after this period. The success of the claim will depend on the prospect of normal working being resumed.

In all cases, to be eligible, the employee must have completed 104 weeks' continuous employment after reaching the age of eighteen, and he must be under sixty-five if a man, or sixty if a woman, by the Saturday of the week in which the contract is terminated. There are reductions in the payment for people who are nearing the retiring age when they become redundant.

A claim must be made within six months after ending employment. A late claim will still be considered by an Industrial Tribunal if it is made within the next six months, provided the employee has an acceptable reason for failing to claim in time. The amount of the payment depends on age and length of service, and it is expressed in terms of so many weeks' pay. The Department of Employment publishes a booklet *The Redundancy Payment Scheme* with a ready-reckoner for calculating the payment due. The maximum figure is £2,400, and the payment is generally not taxable. It does not affect any entitlement to unemployment benefit. If for financial reasons the employer cannot make the payment, the employee can apply to the Department of Employment, who may make a direct payment to him from the Redundancy Fund. If an employer refuses to pay, the employee can refer the matter to an Industrial Tribunal.

Equal Opportunities

It is unlawful for an employer to discriminate against an employee on the grounds of his or her sex, or on the grounds that he or she is married. Discrimination can arise in various ways—refusal to offer a job, offering the job on different terms, denying opportunities for promotion, and so on. It is also unlawful to be victimised by your employer for asserting your rights under the Sex Discrimination Act 1975 or the Equal Pay Act 1970.

Discrimination is *not* unlawful:

1 Where the employment is in a firm which employs no more than five people, although the discrimination will still be unlawful if it takes the form of victimisation.
2 Where special treatment, such as additional time off, is given to women in connection with pregnancy and childbirth.
3 Where being of a particular sex is a genuine occupational qualification for that job. For example, decency demands that the attendants in men's lavatories be male, and persons working in single-sex establishments, such as a men's prison, would be expected to be of that sex. If the work required the employee to live in and the other occupants were all men, a woman could not complain of discrimination, provided the employer could show it was not reasonable to expect him to provide private sleeping or sanitary arrangements for a woman.
4 Where the law prohibits or restricts the employment of women. For example, women cannot work underground in mines.

The equal opportunities legislation has had its greatest effect in advertising. It is unlawful to advertise for a postman, for example, unless the advert makes it quite clear that both sexes can apply. The maximum fine is £400. However, in cases where discrimination is lawful (see above), the advert is not unlawful.

If you consider that you have been discriminated against in the field of employment, you can complain to an Industrial Tribunal. As with unfair dismissal, a Conciliation Officer of A.C.A.S. will be available, if both parties wish, to try to promote a settlement. The maximum compensation which the tribunal can award is £5,200. In the case of advertisements, complaints can only be taken up by the Equal Opportunities Commission, and not by an individual.

Equal Pay

Under the Equal Pay Act 1970 a woman has the right to equal pay, bonuses, holiday entitlement, sick pay, and so on, with a man if she is either employed on the same, or broadly similar, work, or employed in a job which, although different from that of the man, has been given equal value under job evaluation, whereby the employer employs work-study experts to produce a job-grading system. She has two remedies. She can either ask the Secretary of State to have the pay agreement, wage structure, or collective agreement concerned referred to the Central Arbitration Committee, or, more commonly, she can apply to an Industrial Tribunal.

At the tribunal, she would have to establish either that the work she does is of the same or of a broadly similar nature to that done by a man or men, and that any differences between the jobs are not of practical importance, or that the two jobs have been given the same value under a job-evaluation scheme. The employer has a defence if he can show that the variation in the treatment of the woman and the man is genuinely due to some material difference other than sex. The decision of the tribunal can be appealed to the Employment Appeal Tribunal in Glasgow (see p. 116).

Industrial Tribunals

Industrial Tribunals comprise a legally qualified Chairman and two lay members, one appointed from a panel representing employers, and the other from a panel representing employees. They deal mainly with breaches of contract, entitlement to redundancy payment, unfair dismissals, breaches of health and safety regulations, complaints of sex discrimination, applications for equal pay, and cases regarding the right to return to work after childbirth. There is an appeal structure in certain cases, first to the Employment Appeal Tribunal, then to the Inner House of the Court of Session, and then to the House of Lords.

Legal aid is not available for a case before an Industrial Tribunal, but it is possible to obtain advice from a solicitor under the Legal Advice and Assistance Scheme for the initial work before the hearing.

The Procedure

Application forms can be obtained from offices of the Department of Employment, and they should be sent to the Central Office of Industrial Tribunals, St Andrew's House, 141 West Nile Street, Glasgow G1 2RU. The tribunal will usually send a copy of your complaint to the Advisory, Conciliation and Arbitration Service (A.C.A.S.), and an officer of A.C.A.S. will probably contact you to try to arrange a reconciliation. If agreement cannot be reached at this stage, the complaint will be heard by the Industrial Tribunal.

At the tribunal, you can be represented by a solicitor if you wish, or you can present your case yourself, or have it presented for you by an official of your trade union, if this is possible. Representation by an official of your union will be free, and information on any such service will be given to you by your shop steward or a branch officer of the union. The tribunal will not decide the case at the hearing, but will at a later stage issue a written decision, giving full reasons, and a copy of this will be sent to you (unless you were represented by a solicitor, in which case he or she will receive the copy instead).

Hearings before Industrial Tribunals are supposed to be quicker and less formal than proceedings in court, but, in practice, there is still something of a formal court-room atmosphere. Witnesses must take the oath to tell the truth, and are questioned and cross-examined. After the evidence has been given, both parties, or their representatives, summarise their cases.

The administrative machinery of the tribunals is provided by the Central Office of Industrial Tribunals in Glasgow, headed by its President, who is appointed by the Lord President of the Court of Session.

Appeals

If the tribunal decides against you, you have fourteen days within which to ask the tribunal to review its decision, and you can, within forty-two days, lodge an appeal on a point of law with the Employment Appeal Tribunal. This consists of a nominated judge and persons with special knowledge or experience of industrial relations, such as representatives of workers or employers. Legal aid is available for this appeal and, if you have not done so already, you should take legal advice at this point. There is further appeal, again on a point of law, to the Court of Session, provided leave to appeal is granted by the Employment Appeal Tribunal. Legal aid is available for this appeal also.

The Advisory, Conciliation and Arbitration Service

A.C.A.S. is an independent organisation, set up in 1975 to provide advice on industrial relations, conciliation in trade disputes and in certain disputes between individuals and employers, and arbitration services for industry. It is run by a Council which comprises a Chairman and nine members, three of whom are nominated by the Confederation of British Industry (C.B.I.), three by the Trades Union Congress (T.U.C.), and three are independent members.

It has a statutory duty to conciliate in cases where unfair dismissal is alleged, and in other cases involving the rights of individuals under the Employment Protection Act 1975, Equal Pay Act 1970 and Sex Discrimination Act 1975. The Conciliation Officers at the regional A.C.A.S. offices try to help parties to settle these cases. The powers of A.C.A.S. are limited in that no party to the dispute can be forced to go to A.C.A.S. but, in practice, the service provided by A.C.A.S. is widely used and extremely valuable.

Further Information

Local Department of Employment Offices

Central Office of Industrial Tribunals
St Andrew's House, 141 West Nile Street, Glasgow G1 2RU
(041–331 1601)

Advisory, Conciliation and Arbitration Service,
109 Waterloo Street, Glasgow G2 7BY (041–204 2677)

Equal Opportunities Commission,
Overseas House, Quay Street, Manchester M3 3HN
(061–833 9244)

Race Relations Board,
5 Lower Belgrave Street, London SW1W ONR

Further Reading
Leaflets produced by the Department of Employment

Leaflets produced by the Equal Opportunities Commission

Sources of Help
Solicitors

Local Citizens' Advice Bureaux

SOME PROBLEMS OF DAILY LIFE

Our daily lives are closely affected by the law, and it is important to have an idea of one's legal position. We will examine a few of the more commonplace situations.

Arrest

If you are ever suspected of having a committed a crime it is important to have some idea of your rights. The police are perfectly entitled to ask you questions as part of their investigations into a crime, but you cannot be compelled to answer if you do not wish to do so. There are, however, certain circumstances in which you are obliged to give information. The most common of these is where you are the owner or driver of a motor vehicle: you must, if requested by a policeman, give your name and address and that of the driver, if other than yourself. You must also give your name and address if the police find you in possession of a firearm for which you are unable to produce a licence, or if you are being questioned about dangerous drugs.

The police may want you to accompany them to a police station, and it may be difficult to know, at this stage, whether or not you have been arrested, because, in practice, you will generally find that you have little choice in the matter. If you are not free to go, then you have been arrested, and the only way to be sure is to ask the police if they are arresting you.

At the police station, you have the right to remain silent and are not obliged to answer any questions put to you by the police. Anything you do say voluntarily can be used in evidence in court, but the police must not exert pressure on you either to answer questions or to give an incriminating statement. If you are formally charged with having committed a crime, you will at the same time be cautioned that you need not say anything, and that anything you do say will be taken down and may be used in evidence against you. You should never say anything at this stage, as you may be confused and may well say something that you will later regret.

After cautioning and charging you, the police should ask no further questions. Any answers or statements they obtain from you after this point will not be accepted by the court as evidence unless the police can show that they were given completely voluntarily.

On being arrested, you can ask that your solicitor be contacted and the police will do this for you. If he comes to the police station, you may be allowed to see him, but you have no right to insist on doing so, although you are entitled to see a solicitor before appearing in court. The police will also normally tell your family that you are in custody, and may allow you to see a relative or friend.

If the police wish to arrest you, they may do so with or without a warrant. In most cases, if they have been investigating a crime, they report to the Procurator Fiscal who decides whether or not to ask the Sheriff for a court order or warrant for your arrest. You have a right to see the warrant, but a policeman may arrest you even if he does not have the warrant, if he knows that one has been issued.

A policeman may also arrest you without a warrant if he has seen you committing a crime, or has credible information that you have done so, or if you threaten violence, or are seen running away from the scene of a crime. He can also arrest you if he does not believe the name and address you have given him, or if he finds you in possession of goods he believes to be stolen. There are other circumstances which justify arrest without a warrant, but the examples given above are the most common.

You should be brought before the court the following day of your arrest, unless you were arrested on a Saturday, when you will not appear in court until Monday morning. This appearance is commonly reported in newspapers along the lines that 'X appeared in private at Edinburgh Sheriff Court yesterday in connection with the death of Y. No plea or declaration was made and X was remanded in custody for a week'.

When you appear in court, your solicitor may apply for you to be released on bail, a money deposit which you forfeit if you fail to appear in court on the date fixed for your case to be heard. The Procurator Fiscal may oppose bail on the grounds of the nature of the offence, your previous criminal record, the likelihood of your absconding or of your interfering with witnesses. The decision is then left to the Sheriff, who will decide the amount of bail or refuse to grant it. If your case is of a minor nature and will be heard in the District Court, the police themselves may release you on bail, up to a maximum of £20, without your having to appear before a court. Generally speaking, the figures fixed for bail are very low, and in some cases accused persons are released without any bail.

In most criminal cases, the police will not actually arrest you, as the procedure in your case will be summary (i.e. before a Sheriff or Magistrate but without a jury). In such cases, you will, instead, receive a Citation, which will usually be served on you by a policeman, but which may be sent by recorded delivery or registered post. The Citation will tell you the date on which you are required to answer the charge in court, but it will usually also state that you can plead guilty by letter. It will list your previous convictions, and you should check these carefully before pleading guilty by letter. A solicitor can send this letter for you. The letter is also your opportunity to explain any mitigating circumstances which you think might influence the Sheriff or Magistrate. The Citation is almost always used in cases of road traffic offences.

If you receive a Citation and intend to plead not guilty, you must appear in court, with or without a solicitor, on the date stated in the Citation, when a date will be fixed for your trial.

If you are in custody and are due to appear in court, a duty solicitor will be available, free of charge, to represent you if you wish. If, on your first court appearance, you are remanded in custody, your trial must be completed within 110 days. If it is not over by then, you are entitled to walk free.

At a criminal trial, Scots law adopts the principle of innocent until proved guilty. The law demands corroboration, that is, evidence from at least two independent sources, as to the material facts. If procedure is on indictment, the jury will consist of fifteen persons, who will have three verdicts open to them—guilty, not guilty, or not proven. The last is unique to

Scotland, and has the same effect as a not guilty verdict. The decision of a jury is reached by a simple majority. In summary procedure, the judge simply decides whether the accused is guilty or not guilty.

If you plead guilty or are found guilty, you may be admonished (merely reprimanded), fined, placed on probation, or imprisoned. In summary cases, the court may order that you be detained in the court precinct until evening instead of imposing a short prison sentence, but this seldom happens. The court may also defer sentence at the time of conviction, and admonish or fine you at a later stage, when satisfied of your conduct in the interim period. Very occasionally, an accused person will be given an 'absolute discharge', and this does not count as a conviction.

Criminal Offences by Children

The procedure for criminal offences committed by children is different, and is described on pp. 45-7.

Further Information

The Scottish Consumer Council,
4 Somerset Place, Glasgow G3 (041–332 8858)

The Scottish Council for Civil Liberties,
91 West Princes Street, Glasgow
G4 9BY (041–331 2351)

Solicitors

Local Citizens' Advice Bureaux

Further Reading

The Police in Scotland: Your Rights When Searched, Questioned or Arrested—The Scottish Consumer Council (25p)

Road Traffic Law

Legal Requirements for Drivers of Motor Vehicles

1 You must be at least seventeen years old (in the case of motorcycles the minimum age is sixteen).
2 You must hold a current, valid driving licence.

3 The vehicle must be licensed.
4 The vehicle must be insured for you to drive it, at least in respect of third-party risk (death or injury to any person, including passengers, caused by the use of the vehicle).
5 If the vehicle is more than three years old, it must have a current test certificate (commonly called an 'M.O.T.' certificate).

A uniformed policeman may stop you at any time. He is entitled to ask your name and address, to see your driving licence, insurance certificate and 'M.O.T.' certificate, and to search the vehicle, if he suspects that it contains dangerous drugs, or that it has been involved in a crime, and to test the condition of the vehicle. You may not have on you all the documents which the police ask for. If this is the case, you will be required to produce the missing documents at a police station within five days.

It is an offence to disobey a traffic sign or road sign, or a policeman on point duty (unless you can prove that it was a genuine emergency).

Drink, Drugs and Driving

Procedure I

It is an offence, under the Road Traffic Act 1972, to drive, or attempt to drive, or be in charge of a motor vehicle, on a road or other public place, with more than the prescribed limit of alcohol in the blood or urine. The prescribed limit is 80 milligrammes of alcohol in 100 millilitres of blood; and 107 milligrammes of alcohol in 100 millilitres of urine. Unless there are special reasons (see p. 130), the penalty is automatic disqualification from driving for one year, and you may also be fined up to £100 or imprisoned for up to four months. If it is not your first conviction for this offence, you may be imprisoned for six months or disqualified for three years. If the offence is 'being in charge', the judge may, at his discretion, not disqualify you.

The offence has several aspects:

1 You must have driven, attempted to drive, or have been in charge of a motor vehicle before a policeman can require you to take a breath test. It is a defence to prove

that there was no likelihood that you would drive over the limit—for instance, if you had booked into a nearby hotel, or given the keys to someone else, and arranged for him to drive the vehicle for you. It will not, however, do to show that you were too drunk to be *capable* of driving, because you might drive off when you recovered a little, but still be over the limit

A vehicle need not be moving for you to be driving or attempting to drive it—anything connected with the driving is sufficient. To be 'in charge' of a motor vehicle is broader still. Scottish courts have held that a drunk person in the passenger seat was in charge of a car where the driver was a learner under his supervision. You are in charge of the car even if you have had an accident and are too badly hurt to drive or the car is too badly damaged. You are probably not in charge if you have left the car and gone to bed, if you can show that there was no likelihood of your getting up to drive the vehicle while still exceeding the permitted alcohol level.

2 The offence must take place on a road or other public place. The forecourt of a filling station, and a car park attached to a pub are public places, but whether a car park attached to, say, a golf club is public or private depends on whether or not there is public use of the car park. A field used as a car park at an agricultural show is clearly public, whether or not there is an admission charge for parking. The grounds of your own home are probably not a public place. If you are merely sitting there in your parked car without having been in the road the police cannot require you to take a breath test, but they can pursue you from the public road into your house.

3 Only a constable in uniform can require you to take a breath test. He need not wear a helmet, and he may be driving in an unmarked car. A constable in uniform can require you to take a breath test on information he has received from a constable not in uniform.

A constable is entitled to stop you if he suspects that you have committed a traffic offence while your vehicle was in motion, or if he suspects that you have alcohol in your body. Once again, his grounds for suspicion need not be first-hand—he can be called in by plain-clothes officers or receive his information over his police radio. A *moving* traffic offence is not just an accident and covers, for example, speeding, driving without lights, and other offences under the Road Traffic Act. It does not include driving with an unilluminated rear number plate which is a breach of regulations made under the Vehicles (Excise) Act 1971.

4 When stopped, you will be asked to give a breath test 'there or nearby'. A police station $1\frac{1}{2}$ miles away has been held not to be 'there or nearby'. Usually the test is taken at the side of the road almost immediately, although a policeman not carrying a breathalyser may have to radio for one to be brought.

5 It is an offence to refuse to take the test, unless you have reasonable cause for refusing, and the policeman may arrest you for your refusal. The maximum fine is £50. If you suffered from a respiratory complaint that would be sufficient ground for refusal.

6 If the first test is not positive, you cannot be required to give another one, nor can you be asked to give a blood or urine sample.

7 If you refuse to take the test or if your breath sample is positive, the police can arrest you. If due, say, to a bronchial condition you have tried but failed to give a specimen of breath, you may be arrested so that a blood or urine sample can be obtained.

8 At the police station you must be offered a second breath test before being required to give a specimen of blood or urine. The two breath tests must be at least twenty minutes apart. It is not an offence to refuse to take the second one.

9 If the second breath test is not positive you are free to go. If it is positive the police can require you to give a specimen of blood which will be taken by a doctor. If you refuse, you will be asked to give two urine samples within one hour (only the second sample is sent for analysis). If you refuse or fail to give two samples within the hour, you will again be asked to give a blood sample. You must be warned that failure to give a sample makes you liable to prosecution, a fine, and disqualification.

You can refuse to give either a blood or a urine sample, but not both unless you have reasonable cause for refusing. If you refuse you are liable to be punished as if you had been convicted of the offence for which you were arrested. If you are a patient at a hospital you cannot be asked to take a test or provide samples without the consent of the medical officer in charge.

10 It is the result of the laboratory analysis of the blood or urine specimen, and not the breath test, which decides whether or not you will be convicted. You are entitled to retain a portion of the sample and have it privately analysed. The police must offer to supply you with part of the specimen in a suitable container.

11 After giving a specimen of blood or urine, the police can still detain you until your breath test is no longer positive.

12 When the case comes to court, the evidence of the doctor and analyst can be given by medical certificate, provided you receive a copy of the certificate at least seven days before the trial. If you wish, you can notify the Procurator Fiscal, not less than three days before the trial, that you require either or both of these witnesses to attend in person.

Procedure 2

You can also be charged with the offence of driving, intending to drive, or being in charge of a motor vehicle while unfit to drive through drinks or drugs. This was the only offence before breathalysers were introduced in 1967. The police, in effect, have two alternative courses of action when they stop you. The old offence has been retained because it covers drugs (the breathalyser only covers alcohol). The police officer need not be in uniform to arrest you; you need not be given a breath test; and there need be no suspicion of your having been involved in an accident or having committed a moving traffic offence. Again, the offence has several aspects:

1 You are unfit to drive if your ability to drive is for the time being impaired, and this is proved by evidence that you were driving erratically, or that you had an accident at an unlikely spot. It can also be assumed from other conduct,

such as inability to stand or mental confusion—always provided there is evidence of drink or drugs. If you give a sample of blood or urine, the results of the analysis will be important although there is no prescribed limit for the proportion of alcohol in the blood or urine. The level of alcohol does not necessarily prove the offence, but the court will take it into account. If you refuse to give a specimen without reasonable cause, or refuse to submit to a test or full medical examination, this will be used to support the prosecution's case, although refusal is not in itself an offence.

2 When asked for a specimen, you are first asked to provide a sample of blood. If you refuse, you are asked to provide two samples of urine within one hour. If you refuse or fail to supply these, you are once more asked for a sample of blood. You are entitled to be given a portion of the specimen. The provisions on giving medical evidence are as stated in 12 above.

3 Refusal to supply a specimen cannot be held against you unless it was requested by a constable. If a doctor, as part of his medical examination, requested a sample of blood or urine, your refusal to provide either would not be prejudicial to you.

4 The present procedure is always used in cases where the police suspect drugs. If they suspect drink, they usually will, after arresting you, adopt the procedure outlined in the previous section to obtain a specimen. If they follow the previous procedure, however, they must offer you a breath test at the police station, and that test must be positive. If you refuse to take it, it becomes an offence thereafter to refuse, without reasonable cause, to give a sample of blood or urine, and you are liable to be punished as for the offence for which you were arrested. If you are arrested, therefore, *with or without a roadside breath test*, it is vitally important to note whether a breath test is offered to you at the police station, because this will determine which of the two possible procedures the police are following, and whether refusal to provide a specimen is a separate offence, or whether it is merely an item of evidence which will count against you.

6 The police may call a doctor to examine you, and will normally tell you that you can have your own doctor as well. Evidence of a doctor's observations can be given even where you have refused to consent to medical examination.

7 Once again it is a defence to show that there was no likelihood of your actually driving the car when drunk; but again you can be arrested for being in charge of a car, which would include approaching it without having had a chance to actually drive it.

8 If you are convicted of driving, or attempting to drive, while under the influence of drink or drugs, you can be imprisoned for up to six months and/or be fined up to a maximum of £1000. You will also be disqualified for at least twelve months unless there are special reasons (see p. 130). If you have had a similar conviction within the past ten years, the minimum period of disqualification is three years unless there are special reasons.

The position is slightly different where the conviction is for being in charge of the motor vehicle. There is a maximum fine of £500 or three months' imprisonment. Whether or not you are disqualified is at the judge's discretion, but endorsement is compulsory.

Totting-up Provisions

If you are convicted for any of the above offences, and, within the past three years you have been convicted at least twice and had your licence endorsed, a further period of disqualification of at least six months is added, unless there are mitigating circumstances. The previous offences must have been ones for which you could have been disqualified. Other offences for which endorsement is compulsory involve at least discretionary disqualification, so the totting-up provisions are very important.

Endorsement of Licence

If you are being prosecuted for an offence for which you can be given an endorsement or disqualified, you must either deliver or send by registered post or recorded delivery, your driving licence to the court before the hearing, or produce it at the trial. If you are convicted of an offence involving discretionary or obligatory disqualification, the court may order you to take a driving test before your licence is returned.

If your licence is endorsed, you may apply for a new licence without the relevant endorsement four years after the date of conviction (eleven years in a case of drinking and driving).

Motor Vehicles (Construction and Use) Regulations

These lay down, in minute detail, specifications and standards with which motor vehicles must comply. Their scope is extremely wide. Among other things, they regulate brakes, indicators, leaving the vehicle unattended, audible warning systems, mirrors, noise, emission of oil, smoke or sparks, petrol tanks, number plates, reversing, safety glass, seat belts, silencers, speedometers, springs, steering gear, tyres, wheels and windscreen washers. Copies of the Motor Vehicles (Construction and Use) Regulations can be obtained at a modest cost from Government Bookshops (H.M.S.O.).

The maximum fine for breach of the Regulations is £100, and endorsement will also usually be ordered. Endorsement is compulsory if the offence relates to brakes, tyres or steering, unless you can show that you did not know, and had no reasonable cause to suspect that an offence was being committed. Disqualification for any period, and a driving test, may be ordered only in the case of breach of regulation for which an endorsement could be ordered. The totting-up provisions apply if you are convicted of an offence for which you can be disqualified.

Reckless and Careless Driving

It is very rare for anyone causing death by driving to be charged with murder. This would only happen if the car had been used as a weapon. A more common charge would be causing death by reckless driving. On conviction, disqualification for at least a year and endorsement are compulsory unless there are special reasons (see p. 130). The totting-up provisions also apply.

In other cases, reckless, or careless driving are established according to the circumstances. The standards vary depending on such factors as the weather, traffic, or road conditions, and the degree of recklessness, if any, on the part of the driver.

Any person who is injured, or whose property is damaged as a result of your driving, may have a claim against you if he can prove negligence. Evidence that you were convicted of reckless, or careless driving as a result of the incident would be important.

For reckless driving you can be disqualified for as long as the court directs, and, unless there are special reasons, you will have your licence endorsed. If a second or subsequent offence is committed within three years of the first conviction, disqualification for at least twelve months is compulsory unless there are special reasons. The sentences are liable to totting-up. If you are charged on indictment, the fine is unlimited and you can be sent to prison for up to two years. On summary conviction, the maximum sentence is six months' disqualification and/or £1000 fine.

If you are convicted of careless driving there is no limit on the period of disqualification, and unless a special reason is shown endorsement is obligatory. The sentences are the same for second or subsequent offences, and the totting-up provisions apply. The maximum fine is £500.

Special Reasons for not Disqualifying

The special reasons must be special to the facts of the particular *offence*, as opposed to the offender. They might include the fact that, unknown to the accused, someone had laced his drink, or evidence that he was acting in an emergency. It is not a special reason to show that disqualification might result in his losing his job, or that it was his first offence, because these are matters personal to the accused. The courts allow only a narrow scope to the plea that there are special reasons for not disqualifying.

Mitigating Circumstances

The courts have a much wider discretion when considering whether to disqualify under the totting-up provisions. They can take into account all the circumstances when making the decision. If there are any mitigating circumstances, they can choose not to disqualify. Mitigating circumstances include facts relating to the particular offender, such as his previous good character, or evidence that hardship, such as losing his job, would result if he were to lose his licence.

Road Traffic Accidents

If you are involved in an accident in which another person is injured, or some other vehicle or roadside property damaged, you must stop and, if required by the police or any other person having reasonable grounds (for example, the driver of the other car), you must give your name and address and that of the owner (if it is not your vehicle) and the number of the car. If, for any reason, you do not give your name and address, you must report the accident to the police within twenty-four hours. If anyone else has been injured, you must, within five days, produce your certificate of insurance at the police station you specify when reporting the accident.

If there has been injury to any horse, cattle, ass, mule, sheep, pig, goat or dog (other than those in your vehicle or in a trailer attached to your vehicle), the accident must be reported in the manner described above. Note that the list of animals does not include cats. Birds are also not included.

Further Information

Automobile Association
Scottish Headquarters
Fanum House
Erskine Harbour
Erskine, Renfrewshire

Royal Automobile Club
Scottish Regional Headquarters
242 West George Street
Glasgow G2 4GZ

Consumer Law

Making Contracts

Every time you buy something in a shop, you are entering into a contract, even although it will not usually take a written form. If you take goods on hire purchase you have to sign a written contract, and a written lease is also a contract. Contracts are concluded by a simple offer and acceptance, and, if you sign a written agreement, you are bound by its terms. It is essential that you should not put your signature to any document without first reading it very carefully. If you do not understand any part of it, you should seek further advice from a solicitor or Consumer Advice Centre or Citizens' Advice Bureau before committing yourself, even if you are under strong pressure to sign from the other party to the agreement.

The two contracts most frequently entered into in modern life are contracts for the sale of goods and contracts of hire purchase.

Sale of Goods

The law relating to the purchase and sale of consumer goods has, in recent years, received much attention, both from national and local government and from the media, so it seems surprising that the principal statute governing such transactions is still the Sale of Goods Act 1893. This has, however, been amended by the Supply of Goods (Implied Terms) Act 1973. In most cases, the purchaser has no written contract to fall back on if the goods he buys later prove to be faulty, and verbal contracts are extremely difficult to prove. The law, therefore, has stepped in to provide a measure of protection by stating that any contract for the sale of consumer goods contains certain implied conditions by which the seller is bound, whether or not there is, in addition, a formal written contract with the purchaser.

Consumer Sales

The protection covers only what are called 'consumer sales'. These are, broadly speaking, sales by a seller in the course of a business where the goods are of a type normally bought for private use or consumption, and where the purchaser neither buys them in the course of his business, nor gives the seller the impression that he is so buying. In essence, we are talking of straightforward over-the-counter sales in shops, and also of purchases from door-to-door salesmen, mail-order transactions, and purchase of goods reduced in sales. The protection does not cover auctions, or private sales, where, for example, you advertise your car for sale. In such cases the seller is not selling in the course of a business, and the purchaser does not have the benefit of the implied terms. It is also important to note that if you go to cash-and-carry premises and, in order to obtain the trade discount, pretend that you are in business, the transaction will not be covered by the legislation, as you have given the seller the impression that you are buying the goods in the course of a business.

The general rule introduced into contracts of sale by these implied terms is that the goods must be satisfactory. This, of course, is extremely vague, but there are three requirements which must be met:

1 They must be of 'merchantable quality', in other words, as fit for the purpose for which goods of that kind are normally bought, as it is reasonable in the circumstances to expect. An old car bought from a garage or car dealer cannot, for example, be expected to be in the same condition and perform as well as a new car. The goods must not be broken or damaged in any way and, if they are mechanical or electrical, they must function properly.

2 If at the time of the purchase you make it clear to the seller that you are buying the goods for a particular purpose, they must be fit for that purpose, even if it is not the use to which these particular goods would normally be put.

3 If when buying goods you rely on the description given to them by the seller, they must be 'as described', and you are entitled to return them if they are not. If, for example, the box describes an item as being green, and on returning home you discover that it is blue, it is not as described. It is a criminal offence under the Trade Descriptions Act 1968 for a trader to describe goods or

services falsely. An example of this would be describing a car as having only 20,000 miles on the clock when, in fact, it had done 30,000 miles.

If for any of these reasons goods are not satisfactory, you are entitled to return them and to have your money refunded, provided they are still in more or less the same condition as they were at the time of purchase. You may also be able to claim damages for any loss caused by the goods being defective, for example, if a faulty deep freeze ruins the food inside it.

You cannot, however, return goods which were of merchantable quality when you bought them if you have damaged them since that time, or if you have simply changed your mind; nor can you reject goods at a later date because of a defect, if that defect was specifically brought to your attention by the seller before the contract of sale was made. Another situation in which you cannot return goods is where you had an opportunity to examine the goods before buying them and you later complain about a defect which that examination ought to have revealed.

In most instances when you discover a substantial fault which was not pointed out to you at the time of purchase, you will simply want the seller to replace or repair the goods, but you can insist on having your money refunded, and you need not accept a credit note or a replacement or free repair. If the goods are not readily portable, you can ask the seller to collect them, but your complaint will probably receive more prompt attention if you take the goods back to the shop as soon as the fault appears, with the receipt if you still have it, and preferably with a friend who can act as a witness to what is said.

Second-hand Goods

If you buy second-hand goods from a trader you are protected by the implied terms of the Sale of Goods Act, but you cannot expect such goods to be in as perfect a condition as they would be if new, and it may not be so easy to reject them as unsatisfactory. Your rights will depend on such things as whether you paid more or less than goods of that quality are worth, and on how they have been described by the seller. If, for example, you buy a second-hand television, which the shop describes as being in excellent condition, and within a short time it develops a serious fault which was not pointed out to you, and which could not readily have been detected at the time of the sale, you will be entitled to return it and have your money refunded.

These implied terms are your rights in consumer sales, and any agreement which the seller may ask you to sign, which, in the small print, excludes these rights, is ineffective. You should also note that the liability for putting matters right rests with the seller, whether it be an individual or a shop, and not with the manufacturer. You may obtain further protection from a manufacturer's guarantee, but this is in addition to your rights against the seller, and you should not be put off if the seller tries to tell you that the fault lies with the manufacturer.

Trading Standards

Safety Standards

The Consumer Protection Acts 1961 and 1971, and regulations made under these Acts, impose certain safety requirements on particular types of goods, irrespective of any contract between seller and purchaser, and in addition to the implied terms. Among the items to which these controls apply are nightdresses, stands for carry-cots, electric blankets and other electrical appliances. For example, electrical goods must carry instructions as to the colour coding for the flex. It is a criminal offence to sell goods which do not comply with the safety standards, and the Consumer Protection Acts are enforced by the Consumer Protection/Trading Standards Department of the Regional Councils.

Weights and Measures

The Consumer Protection/Trading Standards Department will also deal with any complaints you may have relating to weights and measures, for example, if you are served short measures in a public house.

Codes of Practice

Many trade associations nowadays have codes of practice, which apply minimum standards of service covering dealings by consumers with all members of the particular trade association. They usually cover complaints about the goods and about back-up services. The Scottish Motor Trade Association, for example, have such a code for used cars bought from members of the Association, and the code gives purchasers certain guarantees, dependent on the age and condition of the car. Other examples of codes are those relating to new cars, shoes, electrical servicing and package holidays abroad. The Office of Fair Trading, local Consumer Advice Centres and Citizens' Advice Bureaux can provide advice and helpful leaflets on these codes of practice.

Private Sales

Goods purchased privately must be 'as described', but they are not required to be of merchantable quality, nor need they be fit for any particular purpose that you made known to the seller. It will rarely be so easy to recover your money if the goods are defective. After all, the seller is a private individual and not a trader, and your rights are based on the contract you have made with the seller. The contract will usually be verbal and it may be very difficult to prove that you were both agreed as to the quality of goods being sold. If a defect becomes obvious it is advisable to consult a solicitor at an early stage if the seller refuses to give you back your money or pay to have the goods repaired.

Auctions

Another situation in which you have only limited rights is where you buy items at an auction. Auctioneers are entitled to exclude liability for faulty goods, but this must be made quite clear to potential purchasers either by a statement in the auction brochure or on a notice displayed in the auction room.

Hire Purchase

The law has done much to regulate the practice of hire purchase in order to protect the consumer, and, in particular, to ensure that unscrupulous operators cannot trick you into signing an agreement which you think is a contract of sale but which is, in fact, one of hire purchase. This has been achieved by only allowing the name 'hire purchase agreement' to be attached to contracts which follow a strictly formalised style and contain certain clauses in bold print advising you of the obligations you are taking on and the rights which you have.

The law of hire purchase is contained mainly in the Hire Purchase (Scotland) Act 1965 (which applies where the total price does not exceed £2,000), as amended by the Supply of Goods (Implied Terms) Act 1973. The Consumer Credit Act 1974 is being brought into force in stages and will eventually completely replace the existing hire purchase legislation, but this has not yet happened.

Features of Hire Purchase

The most important thing to notice is that if you buy goods on 'hire purchase' you do not own them until the last instalment has been paid. Until then, they remain the property of the person to whom you pay the instalments. This may be the person who supplied the goods, but nowadays it is often a finance company. Originally the idea behind this was to safeguard the seller in case the purchaser did not pay all the instalments, and to encourage shopkeepers to give credit for the purchase of expensive goods. The hire purchase contract is to be contrasted with the credit sale, where again you pay by instalments, but in this case the goods are your property from the outset. The major practical difference between the two is that if you take goods on hire purchase, you cannot sell them until all the instalments have been paid, as they are not your property, whereas goods bought by credit sale can be resold at any time. It is very important to know whether any particular agreement into which you are entering is or is not a contract of hire purchase, and the law has introduced certain safeguards to enable you to recognise immediately a hire purchase situation.

The agreement form must have a section printed in red pointing out that the document contains the terms of a hire purchase agreement, and warning that you should sign only if you want to be legally bound by these terms. No agreement which omits this section can legally bind you in a hire purchase transaction. The agreement must also list the goods involved and contain a statement showing the full hire purchase price, the total price you would pay in a simple cash sale, the amount of each instalment, and the dates when payments have to be made. Once you have signed such an agreement, you have concluded a contract and are bound by its terms.

The government regulates the minimum deposit which must be put down and the maximum period of repayment by means of statutory instruments. These figures are altered from time to time, but since 23rd July 1976, the minimum deposit has been 20 per cent for most goods, and $33\frac{1}{3}$ per cent for motor-cars and the maximum repayment period is 30 months, reduced to 24 months in the case of motor-cars.

Your Obligations and Rights

Your principal obligation as hirer will be to pay the instalments. However, even if an instalment is overdue, the owner cannot simply take the goods back. He must serve on you a Notice of Default, stating the amount due and giving you not less than seven days in which to clear the arrears. Only if you do not pay at this stage can any provision in the agreement terminating it, or entitling the owner to recover possession, come into force. Even then, unless you agree, he cannot take the goods from you without a court order. Furthermore, if you have paid one-third of the hire purchase price, and then default in payment, or in some way breach the terms of the agreement, the court can postpone the operation of the order requiring you to return the goods, and give you such time as it thinks fit to clear the arrears. This, however, is a matter for the court's discretion and strictly subject to the court's control; and you must remember that this 'second chance' provision is *only* available where one-third of the hire purchase price has already been paid.

If you run into financial difficulties you may wish to terminate the agreement and return the goods. You are entitled by law to do this, and the hire purchase agreement should tell you this. If you want to cancel the agreement, you can do so by writing to the person to whom the instalments are paid. You must return the goods, pay any arrears, and, if you have paid less than one-half of the hire purchase price, you must make up the difference. This is to compensate for the loss caused to the trader or finance company by your terminating the agreement, though a court could decide that a smaller sum would provide sufficient compensation. You will also have to pay damages, if you have failed to take reasonable care of the goods. If you cannot agree on this figure, the trader or finance company can sue you and the court will decide.

This is a summary of your *minimum* rights and you should check your agreement carefully to see whether it contains more favourable terms. Your principal obligation is to pay the instalments, but the agreement will probably place other liabilities on you as hirer. For example, it may stipulate that you adequately insure the goods. Insurance is the hirer's responsibility, even though he is not, strictly speaking, the owner.

Defective Goods on Hire Purchase

In 'consumer agreements' (see p. 132) you have the same rights as you would have in a straight cash sale. The same implied conditions apply. Any clauses in a hire purchase agreement which are inconsistent with, or purport to exclude these implied warranties as to title, merchantable quality, fitness for the purpose and description are void.

Pressure Salesmanship

Consumers are protected from pressure-salesmanship. If you and the other party or parties sign a hire purchase agreement together at the trade premises of the owner, a copy must be given to you on signature. In other cases, where the document together with a copy is either given to you or sent to you for signature, it is clear that the copy you have will not have the signature of all the parties, and a copy of the agreement must then be delivered or sent to you within seven days of the final signature.

If you sign the agreement anywhere other than in the shop or showroom or the office of the finance company—the most common example would be where you sign at home—a copy must be left with you *and* a second copy must be sent to you within seven days of the completion of the agreement. You then have three days, after the date of receiving the second copy, in which to write to the owner of the goods cancelling the agreement. This 'cooling-off period' is intended to apply particularly to the door-to-door type of sale. If you choose to cancel you are entitled to your money back, but you must make sure that, if the second copy of the agreement arrives, say, on a Monday, the notice of cancellation is sent off by Wednesday at the latest. The copies given or sent to you must explain, in red, your rights of cancellation, and give the name and address to which you should send your notice of cancellation.

Ownership

The main feature of hire purchase is that the goods remain the property of the finance company. If you buy goods from an individual, and they turn out to be on hire purchase, you can be forced by the finance company to return them, as they are the true owners; but there is one major exception to this: if you buy a motor vehicle which, it later turns out, the seller had on hire purchase, you can keep the vehicle provided you acted in good faith throughout and had no reason to believe that the person selling to you was not the real owner. *Note, however, that this exception only applies to motor vehicles.*

Credit Reference Agencies

If you are intending to take goods on hire purchase, or are trying to borrow money or obtain other forms of credit, the finance company or lender may consult a credit reference agency as to your credit-worthiness. The agency may have information on you if, for example, you have existing hire purchase commitments, or if you have been taken to court for non-payment of debts. This information can seriously affect your ability to obtain credit. It also may be incorrect.

The Consumer Credit Act 1974 entitles you to ask the shopkeeper or finance company for the name and address of any credit reference agency which has been consulted. You must make the request in writing within twenty-eight days of the time when you were last in touch with the shopkeeper or finance company. You are then entitled to ask the agency for a copy of any file they have about you. Your request must be made in writing and your letter accompanied by a fee of 25p. The agency are obliged to send you the copy of the file within seven days and, if it is incorrect, you can ask them to correct it. If they refuse, or do not reply within twenty-eight days, you can write a note of correction of not more than 200 words and send it to the agency, within a further period of four weeks, asking them to add it to your file and to include a copy of it whenever they send out any information about you.

New Developments in Consumer Law

Unfair Contract Terms Act 1977

This Act which came into force on 1st February 1978, affords further protection to the consumer. Any terms in a consumer contract (which includes a contract for the supply of goods, but not a sale by auction), purporting to exclude or restrict the shopkeeper or trader's liability in respect of death or personal injury resulting from breach of duty shall be void. If you suffer personal injury due to some failure of the trader to take reasonable care or exercise reasonable skill in carrying out his part of the contract, he cannot point to such an exemption clause in the contract with you and claim that he is not liable. In addition, any other terms attempting to exclude or restrict liability to the consumer for breach of duty, or for breach of contract, will be of no effect if a court decides that the terms were unfair or unreasonable.

The Act applies only where there is a contract. Mostly when you buy goods, your contract is with the trader, not with the manufacturer; so you will only be able to sue the manufacturer if you can show that there was negligence on his part which resulted in injury or loss to you. Even if the manufacturer has enclosed a guarantee with the goods you buy, you may still find that the courts will decide that this does not constitute a contract between the manufacturer and you. If, however, the court decides that there is such a contract, the terms of the guarantee then become subject to the Unfair Contract Terms Act. The provisions of the Act apply equally to goods supplied on hire purchase.

The Unfair Contract Terms Act 1977 also strikes at any clause in a consumer contract of sale or hire purchase purporting to exclude or restrict liability for breach of the implied terms of the Sale of Goods Act 1893, as amended by the

Supply of Goods (Implied Terms) Act 1973, relating to title, conformity of goods with description or sample, or to the quality or fitness of the goods for a particular purpose. These are the implied terms described on p. 133. Once again, you should note that you lose the protection of the Unfair Contract Terms Act if you give the appearance of acting in the course of a business, such as pretending to be 'in the trade' when buying goods at cash and carry premises.

Further Information

Office of Fair Trading
9 Hope Street, Edinburgh EH2 4EL (031–225 3185)

Scottish Consumer Council,
4 Somerset Place, Glasgow (041–332 8858)

Consumers' Association,
14 Buckingham Street, London (01–839 1222)

Further Reading

Leaflets produced by the Office of Fair Trading, especially, *Dear Shopper in Scotland.*

Sources of Help

Local Authority Consumer Protection and Trading Standards Departments (departments of the Regional Council).

Consumer Advice Centres (provided by some Regional Councils)

Solicitors

Local Citizens' Advice Bureaux

Court Actions for Payment of Money

It is only possible here to give the briefest outline of the procedure involved in raising an action in the Sheriff Court. An action for repayment of a debt not exceeding £500, or for damages up to £500, or in connection with the tenancy of a house, is called a Summary Cause. We deal here only with actions for recovery of money.

The Summary Cause is intended to be a quick and easy

procedure, which an individual can raise himself. In practice, however, it is not simple, and strict time-limits have to be adhered to. We strongly recommend that you instruct a solicitor to raise the action on your behalf, but if you wish to raise the action without a solicitor there is a useful booklet, *Guide to the New Summary Cause in the Sheriff Court*, published by the Scottish Information Office and available, free of charge, from your local Sheriff Court or Citizens' Advice Bureau.

The Summary Cause begins with a Summons, a copy of which is served on the defender. The Summons and copy have written on them, by the Sheriff Clerk, a date called the Return Day, and the date on which the case may be called in court (usually seven days after the Return Day).

If the defender wishes to defend the action, he must complete one of two forms in his copy of the summons and return it to the Sheriff Court by the Return Day. These two forms are Form **Q** (which denies the claim and gives the ground of defence) and Form **R** (which admits the claim and offers payment by instalments).

If Form **Q** is returned, the case will be called in court and a date fixed for the hearing ('proof'). If Form **R** is returned and the pursuer accepts the offer of instalments, he or his solicitor writes a note to that effect in a book at the Sheriff Clerk's office, and decree will be granted on those terms without anyone actually having to appear in court. If the offer of instalments is not acceptable, the pursuer or his solicitor must appear when the case is called in court to explain the rejection of the offer.

The pursuer or his solicitor has to confirm with the Sheriff Clerk, in the seven days after the Return Day, whether either of these forms has been returned. If nothing has happened, he or his solicitor writes in a book at the Sheriff Clerk's office that he wishes decree to be awarded, and again this is done without anyone requiring to be in court.

If the action is to be defended on the merits (i.e. the defender denies the claim) a proof is fixed. This is a full hearing, with witnesses.

If the sum sued for is over £500 the Summary Cause procedure does not apply—an Ordinary Action, as it is called, is appropriate. This is begun by serving on the defender an

Initial Writ setting out the basis of the claim. The defender has fourteen days in which to lodge a Notice of Appearance with the Sheriff Court intimating his intention to defend. In practice, the defender's solicitor does this for him. If the Notice is lodged, the defender must appear or be represented at the next ordinary court following the expiry of the two-week period, when an order will be made for the defender to lodge written defences within a certain period, usually two weeks, and the action will be continued to a future date. Further continuation may be allowed to enable the parties to adjust their written pleadings, so that eventually they can eliminate all the ground on which they are agreed, and a document called a Record can be prepared, setting out the pursuer's allegations, side by side the defender's answers. The Sheriff then 'closes the Record' and a date is fixed for the hearing.

It will be clear from the above that, to both Summary Causes and Ordinary Actions, strict rules of procedure apply, and either party could lose the case by failing to observe any of these rules. For this reason, we recommend you to take legal advice if you wish to raise an action, or if you wish to defend an action raised against you.

The Summary Cause is less expensive than an Ordinary Action, but the cost of either can be very high, depending on circumstances. It is impossible to give even a rough guide to expenses, though both pursuer and defender may be able to obtain help from the Legal Advice and Assistance Scheme, and may be entitled to legal aid (see p. 148).

Poinding and Warrant Sales

Even although he has obtained a decree from the Sheriff Court, the creditor in a debt is still faced with the problem of obtaining the money from the debtor, who may still not pay voluntarily.

The first step is for the creditor, usually through his solicitor, to instruct a Sheriff Officer (see p. 25) to 'execute a charge'. This takes the form of the Sheriff Officer delivering to the debtor a letter (usually with a photocopy of the court decree) calling for the debt, together with expenses, to be paid within fourteen days.

If the debt has still not been paid at the end of the fourteen-day period, the Sheriff Officer returns with an appraiser, who prepares an inventory, or schedule, of personal effects belonging to the debtor up to the value of the debt, plus expenses. If the Sheriff Officer cannot obtain access to the debtor's house (he will usually call several times if necessary) he has the authority to force entry to the premises.

Only property belonging to the debtor can be 'poinded'. Goods on hire purchase are, therefore, excluded, as are goods held by the debtor on a sale or return basis, or goods owned jointly by the debtor and someone else, e.g. his wife. Other items which cannot be poinded are clothes, tools of trade, beds and bedding, tables, chairs, heaters and other items necessary to allow the debtor and his or her family to continue to live in the house without undue hardship. The Sheriff Officer offers the goods in the Schedule of Poinding three times to the debtor at the value fixed by the appraiser. A copy of the Schedule is left with the debtor. It is a criminal offence for the debtor to dispose of any of the items in the Schedule.

If the debtor still does not pay, the Sheriff Officer, on the instructions of the creditor or his solicitor, obtains a warrant from the Sheriff to sell the poinded goods. The sale is advertised in the local press, and the sale must take place not less than eight and not more than twenty-eight days after the advertisement appears. The sale usually takes place at the debtor's home, and is normally supervised by the Sheriff Officer. The sale itself is conducted by an auctioneer.

The warrant sale is an expensive process, and it is relatively rare. Creditors are seldom prepared to risk incurring the additional expense should the goods not be sold, and in many cases the debtor pays before this stage is reached.

Arrestment

A debtor may have goods or money which are in someone else's possession. He may, for example, have a bank account, but wages are the most common subject of arrestment.

Arrestment can proceed after the expiry of fourteen days from the granting of the decree by the court. A Sheriff Officer, with a witness, calls at the employer's office and delivers a Schedule of Arrestment. At this stage, the employee may agree that his employer should hand over the sum arrested, and he may sign a mandate to that effect. If he does not, and no voluntary arrangement can be agreed between debtor and creditor, the creditor can raise another court action, called an Action of Furthcoming, and the court will order that the money be paid over by the employer to the creditor. Again, such actions are rare, as the threat is often sufficient to persuade the debtor to pay up.

If the sum arrested is insufficient to pay off the debt, another arrestment will be served, and the next week's wages will be arrested, and so on. The amount of wages which can be arrested is one-half of the surplus over £4, so, if the debtor earns a gross sum of £50 per week, £23 can be arrested. The £4 limit does not apply if the decree being enforced is for aliment, rates or taxes, but, in practice, the debtor must be left with sufficient money to live on. Social security benefits cannot be arrested.

Arrears of Rates and Taxes

Rates

Local authorities do not have to raise a separate action against every person whose rates are in arrears. They prepare a single application to the Sheriff, with the names and addresses of all persons who are behind in payments. The Sheriff then grants a summary warrant which entitles the local authority to recover the arrears plus 10 per cent. This warrant is also the authority for Sheriff Officers to carry out a poinding or arrestment of wages.

Income Tax

The warrant in this case allows the Inland Revenue to carry out a poinding and the whole procedure is faster than that used in recovery of other types of debt. The General Commissioners of Inland Revenue can themselves issue the warrant.

Inhibition

So far, we have been considering moveable goods owned by the debtor. Inhibition is the process of restraining the debtor from selling his heritable property (e.g. houses or land). Letters of Inhibition are served on the debtor and registered in the Register of Inhibitions and Adjudications at H.M. Register House in Edinburgh. The subsequent procedure is somewhat complex, but, for practical purposes, the effect of an inhibition is that the debtor cannot sell or do anything else to the property which prejudices the position of the creditor.

Further Reading

Guide to the New Summary Cause in the Sheriff Court— Scottish Information Office, on behalf of Scottish Courts Administration. Copies are available free of charge from local Sheriff Courts or from Citizens' Advice Bureaux.

Sources of Help

Solicitors

The Sheriff Clerk in local Sheriff Courts.

Criminal Injuries Compensation Board

The Board is not a court. It comprises a Chairman and five members, all of whom are legally qualified, and at least two of whom are advocates. They deal with claims for compensation where the applicant, or a deceased relative, has suffered injury or death from criminal violence. An application to the Board is particularly useful in cases where the criminal has not been caught, or where he has no money and is not worth suing. The injury must have caused at least three weeks' loss of earnings, or must be an injury for which not less than £50 compensation would be awarded in a normal civil court action. The decision is made by one member of the Board, and appeal can be made to a larger Board, but there is no further appeal to the ordinary courts. If you do make a claim, and then recover damages from the offender by successfully suing him in the civil courts, the compensation paid by the Board has to be repaid.

An individual can apply direct to the Board on a form obtainable from the Board's office. The Board hold hearings in Edinburgh.

Further Information

Criminal Injuries Compensation Board
10–12 Russell Square
London WC1B 5EN
01–636 2812

Legal Aid

Legal Advice and Assistance Scheme 1973

This scheme is commonly called 'the first £25 scheme' because it covers the first £25 worth of work done by a solicitor on behalf of any person who is eligible to benefit under the scheme. It covers virtually all work done by solicitors, except actual appearances in courts or tribunals. The application form is completed by your solicitor and signed by you, usually at the first interview. The solicitor assesses the capital and income of both you and your spouse, unless you live apart or have a contrary interest, as, for example, in a divorce action. You must be eligible on both capital and income.

Capital This includes savings, the value of any house you own, and other items of value, excluding the furniture and fittings in your home and the tools of your trade. If the total does not exceed £340, you are eligible on capital. This limit is increased if you have dependants.

Income If you receive Supplementary Benefit or Family Income Supplement, you automatically qualify on income grounds. In other cases, you take the total income of you and your spouse (assuming no contrary interest) during the last seven days, deducting income tax and national insurance contributions. Any weekly maintenance payments are also deducted from income, but rent, rates, hire purchase or any other commitments cannot be taken into account. You then make a deduction for dependants, *if they are staying with you*.

If, taking all this into account, your net income (called your 'disposable income') does not exceed £48, you are eligible on income. If the figure is £23 or less, you will have no contribution to pay. Between these two figures you will have a contribution to pay—assuming that you also qualify on capital grounds.

The actual figures are constantly changing. Detailed up-to-date figures can be found in *Guide to Legal Aid in Scotland*, issued free of charge by the Law Society of Scotland.

Your solicitor will tell you how much, if anything, you are required to pay. Your contribution is payable to your solicitor. If his final account does not exceed your contribution, the difference will be repaid to you. If it exceeds your contribution, he will recover the balance of his account from the Legal Aid Fund, which is administered by the Law Society of Scotland. If, as a result of the work he has done for you, your solicitor recovers money on your behalf, his fees will be deducted from the sum recovered.

Legal Aid in Civil Cases

Legal aid covers appearances in court. It is available for proceedings in the Court of Session, Sheriff Court, House of Lords, Lands Valuation Appeal Court, Lands Tribunal for Scotland, Scottish Land Court and Restrictive Practices Court, but not in Industrial Tribunals or Rent Tribunals, although it can be obtained in the Employment Appeal Tribunal. It is available for almost all types of cases, whether you are pursuer or defender.

First you must complete the application form, usually at the office of your solicitor. The form contains a declaration of your means and the income you anticipate receiving in the next twelve months. Any capital you have is taken into account, and the resources of your spouse are also included, unless you have a contrary interest, as, for example, in a divorce action. The application is sent, with a memorandum outlining the nature of the action, to the Legal Aid Committee, and is intimated to the other party to the action. The Committee consider whether you have substantial grounds for raising or defending the action. The portion of the form relating to your means is sent to the Department of Health and Social Security, who will call you in for an interview to verify that you are eligible on financial grounds. If you are eligible, but have a contribution to pay, the Department fixes the maximum amount of your contribution. They consider both your capital and income, and you must qualify on both grounds.

Capital This includes savings and the value of any house you own, but does not include furniture and fittings or tools of trade. Certain allowances are deducted for dependants. You also deduct the amount (if any) by which your disposable or net income is less than £1,200. If the net figure of disposable capital does not exceed £1,600, you are eligible on capital grounds. If the figure is less than £340, you will have no contribution to make from your capital. Between these figures, you will be required to make a contribution.

Income You automatically qualify on income grounds if you are receiving Supplementary Benefit or Family Income Supplement. In assessing your disposable income, the Department makes allowances for tax, rent, rates, and any sums being paid by you for the maintenance of dependants. If your disposable income is less than £2,400 in the year, you are eligible for legal aid on income grounds, but if expenses exceed £760 you will have to pay a contribution of not more than one-third of the excess over £760. If they are less than £760, you will have no contribution to pay.

The figures given above change from time to time. For up-to-date details, see the Law Society of Scotland's *Guide to Legal Aid in Scotland*.

Once the Legal Aid Committee and the Department are satisfied, a Legal Aid Certificate will be issued and the action can begin. The process takes several weeks, but in a situation of urgency an Emergency Legal Aid Certificate can be obtained within about one week. If you have instalments to pay, these will usually be spread over twelve months. The Legal Aid Certificate will not be issued until you have paid the first instalment.

If you are on legal aid and your action is successful, you will usually be awarded expenses. If these are recovered you may have your contribution returned, but if the expenses received, plus your contribution, are insufficient to meet your solicitor's account, you will have to pay the difference. If you lose and expenses are awarded against you, you can ask the court, if you are on legal aid, to reduce the award of expenses to such sum as the court thinks it is reasonable for you to pay.

The legal aid system is the responsibility of the Law Society of Scotland. It is administered by the Legal Aid Central Committee in Edinburgh, with a Supreme Court Committee (for cases in the Court of Session), 16 local Legal Aid Committees (for Sheriff Court cases) and various local representatives.

Legal Aid in Criminal Cases

Criminal legal aid is available for prosecutions in the High Court, Sheriff Court or District Court and in all appeals. An accused person in custody is automatically entitled to legal aid and to representation at the first appearance in the Sheriff or District Court by the duty solicitor.

If you are in custody and plead not guilty, or if you have not actually been in custody but have been cited to appear on a criminal charge, you must apply to the court if you wish legal aid—the application form is fairly simple to complete. The decision is made by the court, not by any Legal Aid Committee.

If the prosecution is a summary case (see p. 11), you must satisfy the court that you cannot afford to pay to defend the charge and that it is in the interests of justice that you be granted legal aid. If it is solemn procedure, then you need only satisfy the court that you cannot afford to pay for your defence. If the court refuses to grant criminal legal aid, there is no right of appeal. There is no system of contributions in criminal legal aid, which covers all the expenses of your solicitor and, where necessary, your advocate.

If you are convicted after trial, you can apply to the Legal Aid Committee for legal aid to cover the appeal, but you must satisfy the committee not only of your inability to pay, but also that there are substantial grounds for appeal and that it is reasonable that legal aid be granted.

Further Information

Legal Aid Central Committee,
P.O. Box 123, 27/28 Drumsheugh Gardens, Edinburgh EH3 7YR (031–226 7411)

Further Reading

Guide to Legal Aid in Scotland—issued by the Legal Aid Central Committee, the Law Society of Scotland (free of charge)

Finding a Solicitor

1 The Yellow Pages, under the heading 'Solicitors'.
2 The Law Society of Scotland, 26 Drumsheugh Gardens, Edinburgh EH3 7YR, who maintain a Directory of Services showing the various types of work done by each firm, and who will refer you to a local solicitor.

3 Solicitors' Referral List, available in libraries, which shows solicitors who handle legal aid cases.

4 Citizens' Advice Bureaux, who will refer you to a solicitor, where necessary.

Further Information

The Law Society of Scotland,
Law Society's Hall, 26/27 Drumsheugh Gardens, Edinburgh
EH3 7YR (031–226 7411)

Sources of Help

Law Society of Scotland

Any solicitor

Local Citizens' Advice Bureaux

Social Work Departments of Regional and District Councils.

IN CONCLUSION

Obviously it is not possible to give you a comprehensive guide to the legal system, but we hope that we have at least drawn your attention to some areas of difficulty. As with anything, half the battle is identifying the problem. Once that has been done it is relatively simple to obtain the correct advice. We have stressed throughout the book the importance of seeking advice before trying to solve your problems. That advice need not come from a solicitor—the Citizens' Advice Bureau is a good starting-point, as is your bank manager, employer or local authority. We have included an appendix giving the addresses of some useful organisations, but the list is by no means exhaustive. Your telephone directory is a useful source of further information, and if all else fails you can always resort to a little detective work of your own to track down those elusive addresses.

Finally, please do not automatically regard this book as a comprehensive and authoritative statement of the legal position on any particular subject. We have tried to include all amendments to the legislation, but there are bound to be changes occurring between the time of writing and publication. As authors, the most we can hope is that we have provided some useful information both for the general public and also for those who cater for their needs and demands. Law is a living subject and one which demands informed criticism and comment.

We would like to thank Mrs Fiona Jack for her assistance with typing the manuscript, and W. Leonard Timson for his help in reading the proofs.

BIBLIOGRAPHY

Coote, Anna, and Gill, Tess, *Women's Rights: a Practical Guide*, Penguin, 2nd edition, 1977.

Gimblett, Margaret, Adler, Michael, Adler, Ruth, and Wasoff, Frances, *Battered Women in Scotland: Your Rights and Where to Turn to for Help*, Scottish Womens' Aid, 2nd edition, 1978.

Grant, Lawrence, Hewitt, Patricia, Jackson, Christine, and Levenson, Howard, *Civil Liberty: The N.C.C.L. Guide to Your Rights*, Penguin, 2nd edition, 1977.

Keith, Richard M., and Clark, George B., *The Layman's Guide to Scots Law*, vol 1, 'House Purchase and Sale', vol 2, 'Divorce', Gordon Bennett Publications, 2nd edition, 1977.

Legal System in Scotland, The, H.M.S.O., 2nd edition, 1977.

Nichols, David, *Marriage, Divorce and the Family in Scotland*, Scottish Association of Citizens' Advice Bureaux, 1976.

Police in Scotland, The: Your Rights When Searched, Questioned or Arrested, Scottish Consumer Council, 1977.

Scottish Legal Tradition, The, Saltire Society, 4th edition, 1977.

Useful free leaflets are published by

Department of Employment

Department of Health and Social Security

Equal Opportunities Commission

H.M.S.O. (*Landlord and Tenant*)

Law Society of Scotland (*Legal Aid*)

Office of Fair Trading

Supplementary Benefits Commission

APPENDIX

Useful Addresses

Advisory, Conciliation and Arbitration Service, 109 Waterloo Street, Glasgow G2 7BY (041-204 2677).

Age Concern, Scotland, 33 Castle Street, Edinburgh EH2 3DN (031-225 5000).

Alcoholics Anonymous, Central Service Centre, 50 Wellington Street, Glasgow (041-221 9027).

Association of British Adoption and Fostering Agencies, Scottish Secretary, 28 West Craigs Crescent, Edinburgh EH12 8NB (031-334 1547).

Automobile Association, Scottish Headquarters, Fanum House, Erskine Harbour, Erskine, Renfrewshire (041-812 0144).

British Insurance Association, Scottish Information Officer, 314 St Vincent Street, Glasgow G3 8XB (041-248 2966).

British Pregnancy Advisory Service, 2nd floor 245 North Street, Glasgow G3 7DL (041-204 1832/3/4).

Brook Advisory Centre, 2 Lower Gilmore Place, Edinburgh EH3 9NY (031-229 5320): contraception and help with sexual problems, especially for younger persons.

Building Societies Association, 14 Park Street, London W1Y 4AL (01-629 0515).

Citizens' Advice Bureaux, Scottish Association of, 12 Queen Street, Edinburgh EH2 1JE (031-225 5323): local branches of C.A.B. can be found in your telephone directory.

Citizens' Rights Office, 132 Lauriston Place, Edinburgh EH3 9HX (031-228 6688/9).

Commissioner for Local Administration in Scotland, 125 Princes Street, Edinburgh EH2 4AD (031-226 2823): receives complaints of maladministration by local authorities.

Consumers' Association, 14 Buckingham Street, London WC2 6DS (01-839 1222): caters mainly for members, but its publications are available to non-members. Enquiries to:

Subscription Department, Caxton Hill, Hertford SG13 7LZ (32-57773).

Criminal Injuries Compensation Board, 10-12 Russell Square, London WC1B 5EN (01-636 2812).

Equal Opportunities Commission, Overseas House, Quay Street, Manchester M3 3HN (061-833 9244).

Family Planning Association, Scottish Region, 2 Claremont Terrace, Glasgow G3 7XR (041-332 1070).

Gingerbread, 38 Berkeley Street, Glasgow 3 (041-248 6840): help for one-parent families.

Industrial Tribunals (Scotland), *Central Office of*, St Andrew House, 141 West Nile Street, Glasgow G1 2RU (041-331 1601).

Law Society of Scotland, The, Law Society's Hall, 26/7 Drumsheugh Gardens, Edinburgh EH3 7YR (031-226 7411).

Lay Observer, 22 Melville Street, Edinburgh EH3 7NS (031-225 3236): for complaints against solicitors which have already gone through the Law Society's official channels.

National Council for the Divorced and Separated, 13 High Street, Little Shelford, Cambridge.

Office of Fair Trading, Field House, Breams Buildings, London EC4A 1P4 (01-242 2858).

Race Relations Board, 5 Lower Belgrave Street, London SW1 0NR (01-828 7022).

Rent Officers: see page 102.

Royal Automobile Club, Scottish Regional Headquarters, 242 West George Street, Glasgow G2 4GZ (041-248 4444).

SACRO (for the Resettlement of Offenders and the Prevention of Crime), 110 West Bow, Edinburgh EH1 2HH (031-225 5232): practical help, advice and befriendment for offenders and their families.

Scottish Association for Mental Health, Ainslie House, 11 St Colme Street, Edinburgh EH3 6AG (031-225 3062).

Scottish Catholic Marriage Advisory Centre, 18 Park Circus, Glasgow G3 6BE (041-332 4914).

Scottish Consumer Council, 4 Somerset Place, Glasgow 3 (041-332 8858).

Scottish Council on Alcoholism, 34 Queen Street, Edinburgh 2 (031-225 1811).

Scottish Council for Civil Liberties, Community House, 91 West Princes Street, Glasgow G4 9BY (041-331 2351).

Scottish Council for Single Parents, 44 Albany Street, Edinburgh EH1 3QR (031-556 3899).

Scottish Health Education Unit, Health Education Centre, 21 Lansdowne Crescent, Edinburgh EH12 5EH (031-337 3251/2).

Scottish Homeless Group, 88a George Street, Edinburgh EH2 3DF (031-225 6167): advice and information on the implementation of the Housing (Homeless Persons) Act 1977.

Scottish Marriage Guidance Council, 58 Palmerston Place, Edinburgh EH12 5AZ (031-225 5006).

Scottish Minorities Group, 60 Broughton Street, Edinburgh EH1 3SA (031-556 4049): concerned with the rights and welfare of homosexual men and women.

Scottish Trades Union Congress, Middleton House, 16 Woodlands Terrace, Glasgow G3 6DF (041-332 4946).

Scottish Womens' Aid, Ainslie House, 11 St Colme Street, Edinburgh EH3 6AA (031-225 8011): refuges, advice, and contact for battered women.

Shelter, Scottish Campaign for the Homeless, 6 Castle Street, Edinburgh EH2 3AT (031-226 6347).

U.K. Immigrants Advisory Service, 47 Cochrane Street, Glasgow G1 1HL (041-552 3773): only between 9.30 a.m. and 1.30 p.m. Advice on immigration law; represented at Immigration Appeals hearings and tribunals.

Widows and their Children, Edinburgh Cruse, 35 Drummond Street, Edinburgh EH8 9TY (031-556 6163): also for widowers. Counselling service and information on various legal matters.

INDEX